CLEAR YOUR MIND THROUGH MINDFULNESS MEDITATION

Discover How to be "Here and Now" Present in The Moment and Let Go. Relieve Yourself From Stress and Anxiety Created by The World Around You

Table of Contents

Introduction 5

Chapter 1: What is Mindfulness Meditation? 7

   The History of Mindfulness Meditation 10

   I have trouble clearing my mind when I meditate. Is it a necessity that when I meditate for my mind to be completely clear? 21

   I'm not good at yoga. Will I still be able to do mindfulness meditation? 21

   Will mindfulness meditation clear all my problems instantly? 22

   Is mindfulness only for those who practice a certain religion? 22

   Is not mindfulness just dealing with positive thinking? 23

   How long will it take me to learn mindfulness meditation? 23

Chapter 2: Getting Started with Mindfulness Meditation 25

Chapter 3: Breathing and Relaxation Exercises 33

Chapter 4: Mindfulness Meditation Exercises 46

   Basic Mindfulness Meditation (Short) 47

   Basic Mindfulness Meditation (Long) 49

   Breathing Meditation (Short) 51

   Awareness of Breath Practice 53

   Breathscape Practice 57

   Mindfulness Meditation for Relaxation and Stress Relief 60

   Mindfulness Meditation for Inner Peace and Calm 63

Chapter 5: Healing Mindfulness Meditation Exercises 69

   Mindfulness Meditation for Anxiety 69

   Mindfulness Meditation for Depression 74

Mindfulness Meditation for Insomnia 77
Mindfulness Meditation for Grief and Loss.................................. 79

Conclusion **83**

Introduction

"With our thoughts, we make the world." – Buddha

Congratulations on purchasing Mindfulness Meditation: A Practical Guide For Beginners and thank you for doing so. This book is all about using the power of your thoughts to be mindful and bring peace, purpose, and happiness to your life.

Drawing upon the rich tradition of Buddhism, mindfulness meditation is all about using your thoughts to be present in the moment and crafting the world that you want to live in. If you want to be more present in your daily life, this book is for you. If you want to heal and cope with chronic diseases, this book is for you. If you want to just sleep better or deal with your depression, then this book is definitely for you. Mindfulness meditation has been shown to have extraordinary effects on your life from your mental to physical health. This book will show you how to tap into the beautiful power of mindfulness meditation no matter if you are Buddhist or not.

The following chapters will discuss everything you need to know about embracing mindfulness meditation in your day-to-day life. However, an important distinction between mindfulness and meditation needs to be made before we proceed. Oftentimes, you see mindfulness and meditation used together. Other times, you may see mindfulness and meditations used interchangeably. Meditation is the more general term that refers to the practice of fine-tuning your mind through various mental exercises. Mindfulness is a form of meditation in which one focuses on being in the very moment compared to other types of meditation practices that may use chants or mantras. For the purposes of this book, it is important to note this distinction. Any meditation practice is great! However, this book will dwell on the importance of honing in on your breath with your mindfulness meditation practice.

Mindfulness Meditation: A Practical Guide For Beginners covers five chapters. In chapter 1, mindfulness meditation will be discussed thoroughly. How key concepts in mindfulness meditation relate to Buddhism, plus the benefits of mindfulness meditation, plus answers to frequently asked questions are included. The subject of chapter 2 is about how to practice mindfulness meditation. A practical guide about which positions are best and other best practices are highlighted. Chapter 3 explores more breathing and relaxation techniques that can be used to bolster your mindfulness meditation practice. The techniques in this chapter are able to help you vary your mindfulness meditation practice. Chapter 4 is dedicated to guided mindfulness meditation exercises that can help you as you begin your meditation practice. The scrips included will help you get started so you do not have to start your meditation practice from scratch. Chapter 5 is also dedicated to guided meditations, but the mindfulness meditation scripts in this chapter focus on guided meditations designed to heal various ailments.

This book about *Mindfulness and Meditation* will more than prepare you to begin your journey into mindfulness and meditation. There are a lot of famous people who practice mindfulness like Naomie Harris, Boris Johnson, Katy Perry, Richard Branson, and Anderson Cooper to name a few; thus, you are in great company.

There are plenty of books on this subject on the market, so thanks again for choosing this one! Every effort was made to ensure it is full of as much useful information as possible. Please enjoy!

Chapter 1: What is Mindfulness Meditation?

> "To think in terms of either pessimism or optimism oversimplifies the truth. The problem is to see reality as it is." – Thích Nhất Hạnh

How many times have we been encouraged to see the cup half full instead of half-empty? Oftentimes in western society, the push to be optimistic and to think positive is drilled into us from a young age. However, if one is beginning to become more mindful, the transition to mindfulness may feel a little jarring as it is opposite of what feels comfortable. Imagine this. Instead of focusing just on the positive aspect of life, mindfulness encourages a realistic outlook on life that embraces the good and the bad, the positive and the negative and the neutral. And this is where our book begins, starting off by learning about this effective way of living that has been used successfully for centuries – mindfulness meditation.

Buddhist monks have been using the power of mindfulness for over 2,500 years. Mindfulness is the act of allowing your brain to rest while observing the thoughts that come and go in your mind. Mindfulness meditation is different from actively thinking and using your creative mind. When you are being mindful, you focus on an object, scene or sound that is calm and then let your thoughts gently amble by in your mind. Being mindful is powerful because if you are always caught up into being busy and always thinking about your next step, mindfulness gives you a much-needed break and makes you reflect on your pattern of thoughts and actions. It is the exact opposite of the daily living experience of most people because instead of going, mindfulness encourages you to slow down the pace.

Mindfulness allows you to know your thoughts instead of trying to change them. Instead of being judgmental and unkind to yourself if you think something negative, mindfulness has no judgment value on your thoughts. Your thoughts are just there. When you are mindful, you are taking notes of your thoughts like a note-taker. When you are in a mindful state, you just pay attention to what your thoughts are doing but giving them the freedom to do what they want. Ultimately, the goal of mindfulness is to know your mind. Once you begin to know your mind, you can begin the next step which is to train your mind.

The beautiful thing about our minds is that they are malleable, and as a result, they are trainable. Our minds are able to change based on what one is thinking. If you think the world is a horrible place, you will operate from a place of fear and your actions will show that. If you think that the world is a wonderful place, you will operate from a place of reckless optimism without being able to be realistic about certain dangers you may find yourself in. Mindfulness helps you to know your thoughts and then begin to train your thoughts to become more in tune with your long-term goals. Mindfulness slows down the grind of your busy daily pace and gives you a different vantage point about patterns in your life. These patterns can be feelings that you have in certain situations or your reactions to how other people treat you. When you are being mindful, you may notice trends and patterns that you are constantly thinking. Are you always wanting more and more? Do you feel comfortable with the way things are? Whatever patterns you notice, mindfulness can help you pinpoint what types of things are causing you mental, anguish, conflict, or joy. Then after noticing these patterns, you can begin to shape it to how you would like to be by focusing on being more gracious, compassionate, and kind with your thoughts.

When you begin your practice, do not treat your mindfulness meditation practices as an obligatory item on your daily to-do list. When you meditate, you want to be present in the moment, not treating the practice as an aggressive measuring stick to how fast you can change or using your meditation practice as a form of escapism without being willing to change your ideals. The most important thing to remember before you begin is that you are training your mind to be at peace with how things are going in the world, no matter what is happening. Once you are able to be at peace in no matter what situation you find yourself in, then you are able to start to work on yourself to change your values. Mindfulness meditation is not a sprint; it is a marathon that you continually work on until you are finally able to free yourself from unsavory emotions that are clinging to you whether they are anger, agitation, negativity, self-image issues, unfair, hasty judgments, and biased opinions and ideals.

When you are training your mind to be more mindful, affirmations are great tools to use. Affirmations are very helpful, especially when you create them yourself. The thought process behind using affirmations is to use very direct language which influences your subconscious to help you get the outcome that you want to get. When you use affirmations, you want to first figure out what outcome it is that you want. Then create a short sentence with an active word. Make sure the sentence is in the present tense. For example, if you want to feel calmer and not be so anxiety-ridden, you can create an affirmation to help. You will start with the outcome of being calmer and make that into a statement using the present tense. Thus, the affirmation would be 'I am more calm.' By using the present tense, you are affirming the future outcome. When the affirmation is created, you can say it during your meditation time and throughout the day. When you couple this practice of saying affirmations with your mindfulness meditation session, they work doubly together to help you get the outcome that you want to get. For example, you hear the term think positive all the time. It is because positive thinking can help shape your future to where you have a positive future. However, if you think negative oftentimes a reality reflects your thoughts. Our thoughts influence our subconscious which in turn can determine our reality.

Mindfulness meditation helps you shape your reality by taking the time to know your mind. Once you know your mind, you will be able to train it and ultimately free it from negative, debilitating thinking. Every step works together. Before you begin your mindfulness meditation practice, know that it is not going to be easy. It will be a journey, but if you are dedicated, you will see a difference in your life.

The History of Mindfulness Meditation

For Buddhists, nurturing mindfulness is the ultimate path to enlightenment. The point of Buddhism is to reach the highest truth by focusing on overcoming the limitations that your body has. Buddhists practice mindfulness by using four foundational truths of mindfulness. The four truths originate from a Buddhist sutta or sutra which is similar to a form of Buddhist scripture. The name of the sutta is called "The Discourse on the Establishing of Mindfulness" or the *Satipatthana sutta*. Please remember that the four establishments of mindfulness come from a very long and rich history. This book cannot possibly cover everything related to them, but hopes to serve as a general overview that can deepen your understanding of mindfulness meditation. The four truths are mindfulness of the body, mindfulness of feelings, mindfulness of consciousness and mindfulness of phenomena. Each foundation normally goes step-by-step in a flowing manner. You can go in and out of meditating upon each truth. They all work together. The first stop on the mindfulness journey is mindfulness of the body.

What is the one thing that you typically hear before beginning any form of meditation? The answer is watching your breath. Most meditation practices or guided meditations instruct you to begin by taking deep breaths in and exhaling deep breaths. Therefore, when you practice mindfulness, the first step is to think about mindfulness of your body. Initially, you'll want to start by being mindful of your breathing. Notice how deep or how shorts your breaths are when you start your meditation session. There are also different forms of body mindfulness you can focus on as well, such as mindfulness of eating or mindfulness of how you walk. These are some of the easiest mindfulness of the body to begin with, but we will focus on mindfulness of breathing since breathing is key to healing lots of ailments, physical and mental in your body.

Mindfulness of the body is just not about the positions your body is sitting in or how you breathe, eat and walk. Mindfulness of the body also involves a deeper understanding of how all your body parts work together. This includes how your leg connects to your thigh, how your ears function, or the power of body working throughout your body. Mindfulness of the body also seeks to understand some of the more unpleasant bodily functions such as urine or snot boogers or blood. The purpose of being mindful of your body is to reflect on how your body functions. You may ask, how do I try to be mindful of my body when I am meditating? An easy introductory way to do this is to imagine yourself greeting and thanking each body part for what it does. You can start at your feet and work your way up until you reach the top of your body.

The next foundation you should be concerned with when practicing mindfulness meditation is mindfulness of your feelings. A better way to explain mindfulness of your feelings is that this truth is concerned about being mindful of your neutral, painful, and pleasurable feelings. You can also reflect on how to be mindful of these feelings by using the senses of your touch, smell, hearing, seeing, taste, and your mind. In Buddhism, your mind is considered a sixth sense. It important to be mindful of these feelings because when you have painful feelings they can lead to fear and hatred. Too many neutral feelings can cause you to become disinterested and floated through life. When you are neutral about something, you are not concerned about it and as a result, it will not be important to you. Lastly, you have to be mindful of pleasurable feelings because too many pleasurable feelings can lead to lust and greed. It is important to be non-judgmental and only observe your thoughts, not acknowledge them when you meditate. The reason you do not want to acknowledge anything is that once you begin to acknowledge a thought as a neutral, painful or pleasurable feeling, you are in danger of attaching yourself to feelings that will prevent you from being enlightened. Thus, it is best to use mindfulness to observe when you are gaining feelings of neutrality, pleasure or painful so you know how to handle those feelings appropriately. When you practice mindfulness of feelings, you will still experience feelings.

Mindfulness of feelings does not mean that you do not feel. It only means that you are able to enjoy the feelings without going overboard to the point of the feelings cause you to become obsessed and overly attached to the thing that is causing the feeling, whether those feelings are good or bad. For example, if you love doughnuts and you find yourself obsessing over doughnuts, you can enjoy them so much that you want more and more doughnuts because of the pleasurable feeling that doughnuts give you. Eating too many doughnuts can cause issues your health like diabetes or chronic inflammation. All of these feelings started because of the seemingly innocent, yet pleasurable feeling of liking doughnuts. On the other side, if you are leery of a certain political leaning and it brings you immense pleasure, attaching yourself to that displeasure can quickly lead to hatred and biased feelings. However, if you are able to know your thoughts and know that this political leaning causes displeasure, you can work to be mindful that the political leaning is a trigger for you without attaching too much to that feeling to the point that it goes overboard. Likewise, if you feel neutral about a person, you can become so disinterested in them that you lose focus of the fact that they are human and worthy of respect. Hence, if they ever needed something, you would most likely overlook them or drag your feet to help them. So even feelings of neutrality can be dangerous. Once you become too attached to any type of feeling, the excess doting on the feeling prevents you from reaching enlightenment.

The next foundation of mindfulness meditation that you want to build upon is mindfulness of your consciousness. In Buddhism, there are 52 mental formations. Mental formations translated loosely are emotions and states of mind. The mental formations are normally grouped together in a specific way. The first of these formations are the previous feelings that were discussed in the mindfulness of feelings consisting of feelings of pleasure, neutrality, and displeasure. The next 51 formations are what the mindfulness of the consciousness helps you to focus on that are clustered in different groups. These include:

- Proficiency of mental properties

- Pliancy of mental properties

- Perception

- Composure of mind

- Appreciation

- Effort

- Righteousness of mind

- Worry

- Desire to do

- Amity

- Psychic life

- Error
- Perplexity
- Feeling
- Right livelihood
- Volition
- Initial application
- Attention
- Greed
- Buoyancy of mental properties
- Adaptability of mind
- Recklessness
- Right speech
- Sloth
- Discretion
- Proficiency of mind
- Modesty
- Conceit
- Right action

- Faith
- Buoyancy of mind
- Pliancy of mind
- Contact
- Deciding
- Concentration of mind
- Torpor
- Mindfulness
- Disinterestedness
- Envy
- Shamelessness
- Adaptability of mental properties
- Distraction
- Composure of mental properties
- Dullness
- Balance of mind
- Sustained application
- Pity

- Selfishness

- Reason

- Righteousness of mental properties

- Hate

This is a general overview of the mental formations, but you can study them in more detail to get a more detailed understanding. To simplify this foundation, when you are practicing mindfulness of the conscience, be observant of the different feelings that go in and out of your brain. To easily start meditating with mindfulness of the conscience, when you meditate observe any thoughts that you have. When your mind drifts from focusing on your breathing, you can call out to yourself that you are being mindful. When your mind begins to drift from not meditating, you can call out to yourself that you are not being mindful. This simple exercise is using mindful of your consciousness. It is also a great trick to use in your everyday life when you want to be more mindful.

The last foundation of mindfulness that you want to build upon is mindfulness of phenomena or mindfulness of perception. When you think of a car, you know it is an object that has four wheels and has the capacity to take you here and there. The idea that you have in your mind of a car may be realistic and based on a car that you know personally. Or the idea of a car that you may have can be based on what your perception of what a car is generally, according to your knowledge of what a car is. When you practice mindfulness of mental objects, you try to focus on the 'why' of how you perceive something. If you think of cars as positive, this positive association could be because of a childhood memory that when growing up you had a wonderful experience of your parents taking you to school every day in an old beat up, yet comfortable car. If you have a negative perception of cars, it could be because your friend was killed by a car or cars cause you to think of all the damage that they do to the ozone layer. Mindfulness of perception allows you to focus on the experiences that shape your perception of what something is so you can bypass those perceptions to get to the true meaning of what something actually is and not what you think something is.

When you practice mindfulness of perception, you want to be aware of things that can cause your perception to be tainted. These can be known as the 5 hindrances. You also want to be mindful of the 7 factors of awakening which should be what you aspire your perceptions to be based on. When all of these factors work together, it helps you eliminate suffering. The 7 factors of awakening that you want to focus on when you practice mindfulness of perception include:

- Equanimity – This factor can be described as the calm observance of things around you.
- Energy – This is the energy that powers you to lead the investigation to seek understanding about different topics in life.
- Concentration – The complete focus of the mind is what this factor seeks.
- Investigation of your perception – This factor encourages you to seek knowledge about phenomena to understand how something operates.
- Joy -Balanced pleasurable interest in something is what this factor is all about.
- Tranquility – Serenity and quietness encompass this factor.
- Mindfulness – Present moment awareness describes this factor.

The 5 hindrances to avoid are:

- Dullness – Doing your takes half-heartedly with no vim or lacking concentration.

- Lust – A craving for pleasure to fulfill all your senses.
- Ill will – Feelings of hatred directed to others.
- Restlessness and worry – This is when you are unable to calm your mind.
- Doubt – A lack of trust or conviction.

When you monitor your thoughts to see if any of the 5 hindrances appear in your train of thoughts, you want to note when and why they arose. You'll also want to note how you can prevent the hindrance from appearing again and how you can replace the hindrance with one of the 7 factors of awakening in their wake.

As you work on your mindfulness meditation, strive to attain the four foundational truths in the order of mindfulness of body, mindfulness of feelings, mindfulness of consciousness, and mindfulness of perception. This is ideal. However, you can meditate upon all of the foundations in one setting as well. So, if you focus on more than one truth at a time, that is ok as well. To truly attain enlightenment, you must find a way to master them all.

Lastly, mindfulness meditation helps you cultivate awareness of the "three characteristics of experience." According to Buddhism, if you do not understand these three characteristics, then you are bound to be caught up into an endless cycle of suffering. The three characteristics you should be aware of are the traits of impermanence, or *anitya*, dissatisfaction, or *duhkha*, and egolessness, or *anatma*. Impermanence means that all conditioned things will change. There is a constant change that you must be aware of. The next trait of dissatisfaction means that there is pain and suffering and no satisfaction in an unenlightened state. *Anatma* means that one should strive to act without an ego. These three are another aspect of Buddhist underpinnings behind the mindfulness meditation practice. These are great to keep in the back up your mind when you are doing mindfulness meditation.

Hopefully, up until this point, the case for why you practice mindfulness has been made. In case you still are not convinced, let's try to convince you one more time. So why mindfulness? There are lots of different meditation practices you can choose from, but mindfulness meditation is a great way to begin for a few different reasons.

Mindfulness is awesome because it:
- Helps you not be judgmental – One of the major components of mindfulness is to not be judgmental of yourself and others. This gentleness towards yourself improves your overall self-esteem. It also encourages self-compassion for yourself and for others.
- Easy and fast – There is no set time to do it. It is super easy to pick up on and relatively fast to do. Your sessions can be as long as they need to be or as short as they can be. If you have a busy schedule, you can meditate for 5 minutes or however long is best for you.
- Reduces stress instantly -Because the necessity of breathing is at the core of mindfulness meditation, deep breathing immediately reduces the stress you may be feeling as soon as you begin your mindfulness meditation session.
- Improves your wisdom – Mindfulness meditation improves your wisdom because you are able to figure out what makes you tick by noting and understanding the power of your thoughts. You also are able to be wise about other people, because this system meditation improves your observation skills such that you will be able to observe others and make connections about their behavior in ways that you have not been able to before.
- No set way to do it – For some people, the fact there is no set structure may be limiting to them, but it is a positive because there is not a right or wrong way to do it.

- Relaxing and calms your nerves – Just like reducing your stress instantly, mindfulness meditation also relaxes and calms your nerves due to the power of breathing.
- Observe yourself in the moment – Mindfulness meditation allows you to be in tune with your thoughts and actions so you are able to get into the 'zone' a lot easier than before.
- Easy to pick-up – Did I mention how easy mindfulness meditation is to pick up? Once you have one session, you will be able to do more rather easily.
- Doesn't have to depend on anyone else to do it – Mindfulness meditation is great to practice on your own. So you never have to worry about if the teacher is going to show up to class or not. This meditation style is self-guided so you can set your schedule according to your convenience.

There are also tons of researched and proven health benefits from doing mindfulness meditation. Mindfulness meditation is a factor in:
- Managing pain that's chronic – Mindfulness helps you strengthen your focus so you are able to focus on other things so that you can manage your paint.
- Reducing anxiety, stress, and depression -Again, the breath and it is healing power makes mindfulness meditation phenomenal at relieving issues with stress, depression, and anxiety. People who practice mindfulness meditation regularly oftentimes have lower blood pressure and a stronger immune system.
- Helps you sleep better -The relaxation that comes from mindfulness meditation helps you hone in on your triggers that help you sleep. It is a surefire sleep aid.
- Helps elderly and pregnant women – Mindfulness meditation does a great job of helping elderly people not feel so alone,

- anyone for that matter, and it is also a great labor tool for pregnant women.
- Improves intuition and creativity – Mindfulness meditation is a favorite of creatives and helps improve the creativity in non-creatives, too.

While there are lots of Buddhists background informing mindfulness meditation, you do not have to practice Buddhism in order to practice mindfulness meditation. This is a common misconception. Do not fret. You may have many more questions, and the chapter will end by clearing up common misconceptions one may have about mindfulness meditation.

I have trouble clearing my mind when I meditate. Is it a necessity that when I meditate for my mind to be completely clear?

No, having a completely clear mind is not a necessity before you begin to meditate. Mindfulness meditation helps you to see your thoughts more clearly. Your thoughts are supposed to trickle along in your mind instead of racing by. Think of mindfulness meditation as allowing your thoughts to go by like a weather scan. They can change minute by minute or hour by hour. Your meditation practice allows you to be in tune with your thoughts. It allows you to keep a pulse on how your thoughts change.

I'm not good at yoga. Will I still be able to do mindfulness meditation?

Sure thing! Mindfulness meditation encourages people to get in a comfortable position before they meditate. For some that may be a popular yoga pose like the lotus pose, but that is not a requirement. Other lie down or sit in a comfortable position. Whatever is the most comfortable position for you is the position that you should use. Also, while mindfulness meditation encourages you to be still, there are lots of moving meditation like yoga or tai chi or mindfulness of walking that encourages movement while you meditate if you ever want to build on your mindfulness meditation practice.

Will mindfulness meditation clear all my problems instantly?

Great question. Mindfulness meditation is not a quick fix. Its power lies in the ability to locate thought patterns and behaviors that may be problematic for you. If you have certain health problems, mindfulness meditation is a great way to cope, but if your symptoms continue to persist, you may need to check in with a doctor for further suggestions for treatment. Mindfulness meditation may not totally eliminate your stress, anxiety or depression, but it will help you cope and manage the situation a lot better than if you were not meditating and certainly without the use of medication.

Is mindfulness only for those who practice a certain religion?

No. You can be any religion and practice mindfulness meditation. It does draw from the Buddhist tradition, but just because you practice mindfulness does not make you a Buddhist, just like drinking wine does not make you a Christian. The great thing about mindfulness meditation is that it can fit in your lifestyle no matter if you are religious or not. If you are interested in adding more Buddhist elements to your practice, feel free to learn more and incorporate it into your mindfulness meditation journey.

Is not mindfulness just dealing with positive thinking?

Mindfulness meditation encourages non-judgmental positive thinking when examining your thoughts, but it does not run away from negative thoughts. Mindfulness meditation also encourages the examination of neutral feelings as well. When you meditate and negative thoughts occur, it is encouraged that you examine the thought and try to figure out where it came from and why you think that way as a way to be able to handle any situation you may find yourself in, whether that situation is positive or negative.

How long will it take me to learn mindfulness meditation?

The journey to learn how to meditation has no set schedule. Learning how to do mindfulness meditation can actually be quite linear. One day you may do well and feel like you're moving forward, yet another day, you may feel like you are going nowhere. One day you will be able to do all the exercises correctly, and the next day you may run into trouble. It is more important to be consistent when you meditate so you can feel comfortable and improve your practice for you to receive the benefits.

To recap, this chapter focuses on the history of mindfulness meditation, which has been utilized by Buddhist monks in the last 2,500 years. The good thing is, you do not have to be Buddhist to practice mindfulness. It couples well will any lifestyle. Mindfulness meditation is built on four foundation truths including mindfulness of the body, mindfulness of the conscience, mindfulness of feelings, and mindfulness of phenomena. A major component of being mindful is being in the moment. Like any skill, it can be learned and improved upon with more practice. Since we have looked into detail about what mindfulness meditation is, now let's get started! Chapter 2 walks you through the first step before your first mindfulness meditation setting.

Chapter 2: Getting Started with Mindfulness Meditation

"When we get too caught up in the busyness of the world, we lose connection with one another – and ourselves." – Jack Kornfield

How often does it feel like life is racing by? We often do not have the time to take the time and smell the roses. We often do not take the time to truly embrace our loved ones just to hug without feeling like we have to rush off to the next thing. In this social media frenzy of a world we live in today, it is easy to lose focus. As a result, if we are not careful, we can easily move like a zombie in our day-to-day lives without fully experiencing everyday life. Thankfully, when you begin to practice mindfulness for just a few moments per day, you will find that you will become more open to the full experiences of life and our daily activities will slow down. And we may, shall I daresay, begin to enjoy life for yourself and enjoy thriving relationships with others to the point that life becomes enjoyable. Yes, mindfulness meditation is a seriously powerful tool that can change your life, but it is also fun! And guess what the fun part is?

The fun part about being a mindfulness meditation practitioner is actually doing mindfulness meditation. Before you begin to meditate, a few ground rules need to be set. Also, a few things should be given as a reminder, too. First thing, when you are being mindful, remember that you are being mindful about something in the present time. The second thing is that for our practice, we will be using our breaths as the center of mindfulness. The more you become aware of what is going on around you and are able to use your breaths to center you, the easier you will be able to experience mindfulness. Becoming mindful can help you break through any biased perceptions you may have, and it may make you feel uncomfortable at times. However, if you are able to make it through the discomfort, you will be able to enjoy it fully. Also, remember, mindfulness does not judge your thoughts or focus on any bias that you may have. It just notes your thoughts as they pass by in your mind until you are able to just let the thoughts be. Your thoughts are not good or bad. You are merely a video recording nothing that you see. Mindfulness helps you experience real-time in super sharp focus. The more you dedicate to focusing on being mindful, the more your mindfulness muscle will be developed, and the easier doing mindfulness meditation will become

The very first thing you should do before practicing mindfulness meditation is to set a pin in your busy schedule that's going to be dedicated to your meditation practice. This is very important. When you set this time, please be consistent. Make sure that this time is distraction free with no person or task able to distract or interrupt you. If you need to set an alarm to remind you, do so. If you need to set your phone on do not disturb, do so. It is important for you to take this seriously if you want to get good at it. To help you set yourself up for success, stick to the time you want and do not let anything get in your way.

When you first begin, it is normal that you may feel a bit weird. Hence, to help you acclimate to the process faster, try to meditate more than one time per day. You can try to have a meditation session at least two times a day. To help make the transition easier, you can try to meditate at the same time every day, but if you aren't able to do that it is okay. Worst-case scenario: on that day you want to meditate, but you are unable to, try to make up the time that you missed. If you absolutely have no time to spare in your super-jam-packed schedule, you can try to meditate while doing another activity. If this is the route you must take, when you are doing the other activity, focus on doing the activity and make note of the thoughts that pass through your mind while you are meditating. For example, you can try to meditate while cooking. When you meditate while doing an activity, make sure that you are doing the activity for its value, not for some other end. For example, if you are cooking, you are cooking because the cooking is an activity, not because you begrudgingly have to cook for your family. Another time people like to meditate is while driving, especially if they have a long commute. Just be careful not to get too relaxed that you lose focus behind the wheel!

Another way to ease into your meditation practice is if you start off meditating in 5-10 minutes increments, at least twice a day, then work to increase your time. If you are having a difficult time even with the 5-10 minutes, you can start off by dedicating just 60 seconds a day and build from there. If you find the 60 seconds challenging, cut it down to 30 seconds and build from there. I cannot stress the importance of whatever you select, commit to it, because if you are able to commit at least 11 days of meditation, your mindfulness meditation habit is more likely to stick than if you did not do at least 11 days.

Something else to consider before you set your time is to consider the time of day that you want to meditate. For some, doing an early morning session sets the tone for the rest of your day. If they can meditate in the morning, they find that the rest of their day goes smoothly. They experience less anxiety and frustration. They remain calm and peaceful throughout the day. For others, the best time to meditate is not in the morning, but the reverse time. Some find that when they mediate after a long day of work, they can decompress from the day's stress and be set up to begin a brand-new day. When they meditate at night, they can sleep better because they are more relaxed and have put their stress to the side. Others still prefer to meditate in the mid-day. This allows them to settle down from the hustle bustle of the day and then prepare them to finish the rest of the day out strong. They also find that a quick afternoon meditation session reinvigorates them and gives them a much-needed energy boost in a much healthier way than eating sugar or drinking caffeine. Not to mention they do not experience any crashes either. I suggest trying every time to see which time is better. If you want to take your practice to the next level, commit to meditating at least twice a day to see how that affects you.

The second step you want to do before you begin meditating is to find the place where you will be meditating. When you find the place, hook it up or customize the place to your liking. For greater comfort while meditating, you can consider purchasing a meditation pillow to sit on or lie on. If you want to save money, you can use what you have around the house, like comfy pillows that you already have around. You can use a comfortable blanket or shaggy rug, as well. Once you select your place, you will also want to make sure that the place is free of distractions. If there is a computer or television or tablet or phone nearby, be sure to put it out of your sight so you cannot be distracted by it. If there is a place to plug your phone in nearby, do not charge your phone in your meditation place. I guarantee you that when you begin to meditate your phone will become a huge distraction. The saying 'Out of sight, out of mind' is definitely true! When you are selecting your room, consider the placement of the room in relation to your house and outside. You want the room to be quiet. There's nothing more distracting than trying to meditate and you have a huge noise to overcome, like an ambulance or fire truck passing in the background. Sometimes it is impossible to eliminate noise completely but try to eliminate as much noise as you can. In your meditation room, make sure that the room temperature is comfortable for you. You do not want it too hot that you're uncomfortable and sweating or too hot that it makes you groggy. You also do not want the room temperature too cold that you are unable to move your fingers and toes.

Once you have your time selected, and your special place decorated to your liking, it is time to meditate. On the day that you want to meditate, you want to figure out the best position that you want to be in throughout the session. One of the most popular poses is called the lotus pose. It is an advanced yoga pose and requires some flexibility. It is the one pose you most often see people in when they are meditating. Before you begin, you will want to stretch. To get into lotus pose, you'll want to be seated on the floor and have your spine straight. Let your arms rest by your side. Then you will want to bend your right knee and bring it to your chest. Then, drop your right ankle on the crease in your left hip so your right foot sole is facing the sky. The top of your foot should be resting on your hip crease. Next, do the same thing on the other side. Bend your left knee and put your left ankle on top of your right shin so your left ankle is crossed over the top of your right shin. Your left foot sole should also be facing upwards and the top of your ankle and foot should be resting on your right hip crease.

Once you are in this position, bring your knees into your body as close as possible while sitting as straight as possible. Your groin should also be as flat and close to the ground as possible. You'll want to put your hands on your knees with your palms facing up. Then create a circle with your thumb and index finger and leave the rest of your fingers extended. Lotus pose can be challenging for those with limited flexibility or those who are just beginning to yoga. The good thing is that there are other positions you can try using if Lotus Pose is a challenge for you. You are able to sit on the floor with your knees bent and legs crossed over each other. You can also just sit in a chair or lie down. The most important thing is to find a position that is comfortable for you.

Once your time is selected, your space is ready, and your position is selected, it is time to begin meditating. When you are in the most comfortable position possible, try to let your body feel loose. You can do this by rolling your neck and arms and shoulders in a circle. You can also stretch the muscles in your face by making a full smile and then a half smile. As you get loose, if you have any tension feel it roll away. Next, you'll want to make sure that your posture is top-notch. Keep your back and neck as straight as possible. Try to keep your stomach relaxed. To take your posture up another level, you can tilt your chin down slightly. Using the correct postures will allow your breaths to be as deep as possible and you will be able to draw in deeper breaths. After your posture is checked, you can then figure out what to do with your hands if you are not doing lotus pose. Your hands can rest on top of your lap, to the side of you on the floor or on top of one another on your knees with your palms up. The next decision you have to make is to decide what to do with your eyes. You can decide to keep them open, half-closed or closed completely. If you decide to keep them closed, be sure not to fall asleep when you are meditating. If you are afraid you may fall asleep, it may be best to keep your eyes open or at least half-open.

Next, focus on your breathing. First, just observe your breath. Remember, breathing is the key to helping you concentrate throughout the meditation exercise. As you breathe, you can notice your chest going up and down. Breathe in through your nose and exhale through your mouth. It is totally ok to breathe through your mouth if you have to. Once you have observed your breath, you can then begin to count your breaths. When you breathe in through your nose and then exhale through your mouth, count it as one breath cycle. Try to count to 5, which would be five completed breath cycles of inhaling an exhaling. Then try to get to 10 with your breath cycles. It should go like this: Inhale-one. Exhale - two. Inhale – three. Exhale- four. If any thought interrupts you, start the count over again until you are able to reach 10 complete breath cycles. This is a wonderful breathing exercise to do when you begin. Now remember, you are just starting so it may be difficult to retain your concentration and that's ok. Be patient, kind and gentle with yourself. If you do find yourself losing focus, the most important thing is to get back on focus as soon as you lose focus by concentrating on your breaths. Keep practicing this until you are able to count to 10 breath cycles with ease.

Then the next step to take your breathing to the next level is to begin counting your inhales and exhales as 1 complete breath cycle. It would look like this: Inhale – one. Exhale – one. Inhale – two. Exhale – two, and so on and so forth until you are able to reach 10 with ease. Once you are able to do that, then you can begin to focus on your breath only. This may take a while, and that's ok. You also may have trouble completing focusing on your breath, and that's ok as well. If you have a thought to interrupt your concentration on your breathing, observe the thought and then begin to count again. The easier you are able to control your breath, the easier your mindfulness meditation will be. Then you can start meditating while doing other activities until mindfulness just become of your daily life.

So, what happens if you are unable to still your mind? That's ok. Keep practicing until you get better. What happens if you are unable to sit in the lotus position? That's ok as well. Find the most comfortable position for you and then go from there. What is I'm unable to be nonjudgmental with thoughts that arise? Guess what? This will take time as well. As long as you are dedicated to improving your meditation practice every time you do it, you are making progress. The more you do it the easier it will be. This is a lifelong commitment so do not feel like you have to be perfect starting out.

This chapter has given you a wide overview of how to get started with mindfulness meditation. As a recap, before you begin your mindfulness meditation practice, make sure that you have already committed to a consistent time that you will meditate in order to build your practice. Try to start off at least five minutes twice a day for at least 11 days so you can build a habit. Once your time is selected, you will want to make sure your special meditation place is specific to you and your needs and most importantly, free of all distractions. There are a variety of positions you can take when meditating, just be sure to choose one that is most comfortable for you, whether it be lotus pose, sitting down, lying down, or standing. When you do begin to meditate, focus on your breathing. Be non-judgmental about thoughts that may float by. If you do find yourself being distracted, bring your attention back to your breathing. More importantly, be gentle with yourself and remember that the more you practice, the better you will become. The next chapter will focus on more detailed breathing and relaxation techniques that can help improve your mindfulness meditation practice.

Chapter 3: Breathing and Relaxation Exercises

> "There is something wonderfully bold and liberating about saying yes to our entire imperfect and messy life." – Tara Brach

Let's face it. Life is not pretty. As a matter-of-fact, sometimes life can get downright ugly. Bills are always due, every two weeks. Relationships aren't always going as planned. And sometimes we just don't like ourselves. On the flip side, there are times where we can feel like we are soaring above the sky with happiness. There are times when we can do no wrong and it feels like life is going exactly as planned. However, the beauty in life is the embrace of both the good and the bad and the neutral. No matter what situations may happen to us in life, we can also count on our breathing and mindfulness to make the most of it.

Since the basics of mindfulness meditation were covered in Chapter 2, it is now cover breathing and relaxation tips that can help bolster your mindfulness meditation practice. As you nail down the basics of your breathing that were covered in the previous chapter, the exercises in this chapter will help you vary the breathing methods you use in your meditation session. The purpose of this chapter is to bring for all the different types of breathing and relax methods you can use to better your mindfulness meditation practice. This chapter will begin by exploring breathing techniques, some used in the yoga meditation tradition, and then will switch focus to relaxations techniques which will bring the chapter to a close.

In yoga, the Sanskrit word *pranayama* means breath. If you practice yoga or if you do not, then you must understand that at the core of both activities is breathing. Steady, deep breathing centers the practitioner in yoga and in mindfulness meditation. In this chapter, seven yoga breathing techniques that will be examined that can help you with your breathing in your mindfulness meditation sessions. As you listen about each one, take notes or memorize about which ones you would like to incorporate into your meditation sessions. The more you try, the more varied and fun your practice will be.

The first breathing technique is called Lion's Breath. It is an easy and fun breathing exercise to do. It does require you to be rather loud, so make sure that you warn the people around you if necessary. To begin, you'll want to be in your comfortable position. You can either be sitting in a chair, in lotus pose or lying down. When you're comfortable, inhale as deeply as you can through your nose. Then lift your arms up with your hands extended and breathe out loudly through your mouth, like a roar. When you breathe out, make the 'haa' sign like you trying to fog up a car window. You can also stick your tongue out when you exhale, too. Lion's breath is a great breathing exercise to relieve tension in your mouth and jaw. It also helps stimulate the muscles in your throat.

The next breathing exercise you want to try out is a popular meditation breathing exercise. It is known as 'bee breath' or *bhramari ranayama*. For this exercise, you need to be in your comfortable position and put your fingertips on your temple. Next, breathe in deeply from your diaphragm and when you exhale out, hum loudly like a 'humming bee.' Do this for a minimum of three breath cycles. This exercise is very helpful at getting your concentration back when you are having trouble focusing. And it is fun, too.

The name of the next exercise is called 'bellows breath.' It is great breathing exercise to do when you need a boost of energy. You also need to be loud for this breathing exercise, so be in a space where it is ok to be loud. To begin, make sure you are comfortable in your space. Then you want to raise your hands in the air like small fists. When your hands are in the air, you can spread your fingers out, too. Next, breathe in deeply through your mouth and every time you exhale bring your elbows close to your body and make a 'HA' sound from your diaphragm. This exercise should be done at a minimum of 3 breath cycles for as many times that you would like.

The 'breath of fire' is the next breathing exercise. This breathing exercise is great for bringing warmth to your body as well as detoxing your body. Just like any other breathing exercise, you want to begin by being in your comfortable position. You want your arms to be resting comfortably by your side. Once you are set, take a deep breath through your nose. When you exhale, instead of exhaling through your mouth, you want to exhale through your nose. But instead of a regular exhale, pump your exhales out through your nose in short sports and pull in your stomach while you do. Do the exhale quickly and make sure that when you inhale again, the exhales match your inhales in time, depth, and force. A similar breathing exercise to this one is called the 'skull cleanser.' It also raises your energy levels. Get comfortable first. This time when you breathe in, instead of putting your elbows to your sides, raise your arms up when you exhale. You still want your inhales and exhales to be done in short spurts, as well as, making sure that the inhales and inhales match in time, depth and force.

The next breathing exercise is one of the most common breathing techniques called the *ujjayi* breath. Before you begin, be in a comfortable position. You will then inhale by using your nose and then exhale by using your nose. However, when you inhale, you want the breath to drag at the back of your throat like you are drinking a beverage with a straw so that a hissing sound is made. You want to extend both your inhales and exhales out until both your inhales and exhales are deeper and smooth as possible. Start the exercise with a deep inhale and let each breath cycle deepen in intensity.

Kumbhaka is the next breathing exercise and its purpose is to help you retain your breath so you can perform deeper inhales. This breathing exercise focuses on the space between an inhale and exhale when you breathe. When you breathe in your nose and then exhale out of your nose pause before you take the next breath cycle. When you inhale, try to keep the breath at two counts, when you exhale, try to exhale at two counts and then when you hold your breath in between the next breath, hold your breath for two counts. After you do this one time, do a regular inhale and then exhale. Then try to do the breath cycle again when you hold your breath after you complete one breath cycle. This exercise can be combined with the *ujjayi* breath in the previous paragraph. *Kumbhaka* is a great warm up before you get deep into a mindfulness meditation session because it helps you set the tones for deeper inhales.

Now we are going to focus on breathing exercises that are not specific to the yoga meditation tradition. The first technique is called left and right nostril breathing. This technique is interesting because, at any time, we inhale and exhale through one nostril more times than the other nostril. This pattern changes every 90 to 150 minutes. Our nostrils are connected to opposite sites of our brains, so our left nostril is connected to our right nostril and the right nostril is connected to the left side of the brain. This technique is great breathing exercise, but it also helps you deal with qualities associated with the particular nostril. For example, the left nostril connects to the right side of the brain is associated with sensitivity, synthesis, calmness, empathy, receptive and cleansing energy. The right nostril connects to the left side of the brain and is associated with concentration, vim, willpower, gumption, alertness, warmth and nurturing energy. To do the exercise, you want to put your right thumb over your right nostril and then inhale solely through your left nostril. Then take your ring finger and put it over the left nostril so you can exhale out of the right nostril. Then keep your fingers there to inhale in your right nostril, then switch fingers and cover the right nostril so you can exhale out your left nostril. Then repeat on each site. This exercise can be tricky so be careful to take note of which nostril you are inhaling and exhaling out of to prevent confusion. This exercise is great for helping you to gain clarity and sharpen your discipline skills.

Equal breathing is another important foundational breathing exercise to know. We've already covered it somewhat but did not mention the specific name. For equal breathing, you get comfortable and then inhale through your nose for 3 counts and then exhale from your nose for a minimum of 3 counts. The important part of equal breathing is to remember to inhale the same number of counts on every inhale and inhale. You can do more than 3 counts of breathing, just make sure that you do the same count on each side. Abdominal breathing or diaphragmatic breathing is at the crux of your breathing exercises. It is also called deep breathing, and it is simply a deep breath that draws from your diaphragm rather than your chest. If it feels weird to breathe from your diaphragm, you should practice diaphragmatic breathing. This method helps your inhales get deeper. You can also put one hand on your chest and another hand on your ribcage to make your breathing deeper. Doing this allows you to feel your breath going in and going out. This breathing technique also helps prevent you from breathing through your chest only. By breathing through your diaphragm is improves your lung and digestive functions, too.

The next awesome breathing exercise is called 4:7:8 breathing. This exercise is similar to the *kumbhaka* breathing exercises that we have named before. For the 4-7-8 breathing exercise, you get comfortable. Then begin by exhaling through your mouth and try to make a 'whoosh' sound. Next, you will need to begin to inhale through your mouth. Close your mouth from the previous exhale and when you inhale, hold the inhaled breath for at least to the count of four which you will count in your mind. Next, hold your breath for 7 seconds. If you are initially unable to start at 7 seconds, that's ok. Hold your breath for as long as possible. Then exhale again, but this time make the 'whoosh' sound to the count of eight in your mind. You can make the breath slow and steady so it can last to the full eight counts. The entire sequence is considered one breath. It is best to start slow with this exercise then increase the speed. When you begin, try to keep the 4:7:8 count as close as possible so you can nail the correct breathing technique.

Since we've discussed breathing exercises, now it is time to begin discussing relaxation exercises. Relaxation is important because it helps heal your anxiety and depression. It improves your skin and your heartbeat and breathing which in turn improves your overall reaction to chronic stress. Without proper rest and relaxation, your body begins to break down because you have no way to rejuvenate yourself. While you may be good at the breathing exercises, your brain may still have racing thoughts. By coupling the relaxation methods with your breathing exercises, you are able to add another layer of stillness to your meditation practice which will make you more aware and present in the moment.

The first relaxation exercise is called autogenic relaxation. The concept behind autogenic relaxation is that you have everything your body needs to relax. (Autogenic means self-regulation or self-generated.) With this method, you visualize that your body is warm and relaxed. The autogenic relaxation method is great for stabilizing your heartbeat, relaxing your entire body and helping you achieve deep breathing. The method is easy. You first begin by finding a nice comfortable place to relax. Then you mentally work your way through visualizing warmth or calmness coming to every part of your body. The warm and calm feeling helps you feel relaxed like you are in a cozy blanket. Begin from the top of your body and work your way down or begin at the bottom of your body and work your way up.

For example, when doing at autogenic exercise (going from the top of your body to the bottom of your body), you begin by feeling relaxed in your head. You can imagine that your head is experiencing a wonderful burst of calm and loving warmth. Then imagine that the feeling of warmth has made its way to your forehead area. You can feel the warmth cause your forehead to tingle and melt all your tension away. Next, you'll want to follow the warm feeling all the way down to your stomach area. Repeat to yourself that your stomach is warm. Then feel the warmth travel down your legs, thighs, shins, and toes, warming every part until you get to the bottom of your feet.

While doing this type of exercise, you can also turn your attention to your breathing at any time. Note how calm and energy-giving your breaths are. You can also focus on your heartbeat and note how steady your heartbeat. It is also great to feel how your heartbeat sends warmth and relaxation throughout the rest of your body, especially your extremities like your arms and legs. Other phrases (or variations thereof) you can say while doing an autogenic meditation are that 'I feel relaxed.' or 'My body feels calm and quiet and comfortable.' or even 'I feel the warmth radiating throughout my body which relaxes and calms me.' (These are a few phrases that can help you get started.) Once you finish, imagine yourself doing an activity that you love. Whether that is relaxing on the beach or playing on the playground with your inner child. The ending activity can even draw on a dear memory that made you feel loved, safe or confident. The ending thought is a comfortable way to transition from the total feeling of relaxation of the autogenic exercise back to your day-to-day life.

The visualization technique is the next form of mental exercise that you can use to relax. This exercise is also fun to do because it requires that you use your imagination. Do you remember when you were a kid and you always used your imagination? It seems like the use of imagination gets lost the older we become. However, with this visualization exercise, you're able to tap into your imagination part of your brain and go back to using your imagination like in your childhood days. A visualization meditation session is similar to daydreaming in that you think of images that may you feel happy.

However, visualization is active and present in helping you figure out how to relax your body by using your senses to think of imagery that helps you relax. Normally, daydreaming usually takes into account memories that make you feel good, whereas, a visualization exercise would observe a negative memory, make note of it, and then return back to the more pleasant feeling. A visualization exercise is also different from a guided meditation because you are in charge of finding the memories of what you're most comfortable with instead of relying on the guided meditation to help you visualize images that help you relax. Lastly, and distinctly, a visualization meditation exercise draws upon all of your senses of touch, taste, seeing, hearing and smelling to visualize the most relaxing moments to so that you can experience a state of relaxation for your entire body.

To begin a visualization exercise, you first must find a comfortable position in your special place. Once you are comfortable, think of an image that makes you feel warm and relaxed. This image can be of you walking on the beach. You can imagine the warm wind whipping at your hair or the warm sun extending its warmth over your body. You can smell the fresh scent of the ocean spray and accidentally taste the salty spray of the ocean as you dip into a way. You can hear seagulls loudly cawing in the turquoise blue sky while the gritty sand can be between your toes. While you are visualizing, do not forget to breathe deeply. You can inhale through your nose and exhale through your mouth. After you finish one visual image, you can transition into a different one. Do not feel like you have to stick to one visualization throughout your meditation session. You can transition back and forth between different imagery.

For example, after visualizing a peaceful beach scene, you can transition to a visual image of you sitting at a holiday dinner table surrounded by family members and friends that you love. The scents of your favorite foods fill the air. Foods like freshly baked bread, cheesy macaroni and cheese, roasted chicken and your favorite desserts fill the air. You can even smell the scents of your favorite person, whether it's leathery, fruity or more flowery. What other scents do you smell? After you work through one sense, like smell, you'll work through all the rest of the senses. How does the food taste when you eat it? Do your taste buds explode from goodness? Does the air taste warm from the heat in the kitchen? How does your clothing feel against you? Are you wearing your favorite blouse or shirt? Are you wearing jeans or some other type of material? Visualize the tight embrace from your grandma or parents. And what about the sounds? How loud is your aunt and uncle's laughter? Imagine the gentle cry of a newborn recently born into the family. How about the holiday playlist playing your favorite songs? Or imagine the lacy detail of the holiday tablecloth. What does the overall scene look like? Who are you sitting next to at the table? If you do not sit at a table, how is the seating arranged? You can be as detailed as you would like as you go through the scene in order to get as many great memories during your visualization session. You can also go as fast as you would like or as slow as you like. Choose to end the visualization on a very happy memory and feel how relaxes your body is. Then take a deep breath and open your eyes so you can go about your day. This exercise is very helpful in helping you relax, and it is one of my favorite relaxation methods to use. You can also couple a visualization meditation session with the use of with affirmations, especially if you already have a list of affirmations written. For example, after each image you visualize, you can say to yourself, 'I am relaxed.'; 'I am calm.' or 'I am happy.' after seeing it. You can also use your affirmations to visualize an outcome that you would like. If you are trying to reach a goal, you can visualize what it looks like when you reach the goal. Use all your senses to imagine the scene and use your affirmations after each scene as well.

For example, if you have a goal of receiving a promotion, you can do a visualization session of you receiving the promotion. Imagine how your boss' office will look like when you get the promotion. How does the office smell? What are you going to smell like? Will you have your favorite scent on? What will you eat for breakfast that day? Will your palms be sweaty? What will your celebration party look like? How will your friends, family, and coworkers act? After each image, say an affirmation, like, 'I work hard, and I am worthy of a promotion.' 'I can do anything I put my mind to.' to name a few. Remember, the more detailed you are, the more helpful the session is. This is a powerful tool to have in your meditation arsenal.

The last relaxation technique examined in this chapter is called progressive relaxation. Progressive relaxation is also known as body scan meditation. The technique behind progressive relaxation is to relieve your anxiety levels, too. This method of relaxation is powerful because when your body is physically relaxed you cannot be anxious. If you are experiencing an anxiety attack or feeling anxious, by the end of a progressive relaxation session, your anxiety should be gone, and your body should be completely relaxed. If you have chronic anxiety, this tool helps you relieve the anxiety outside of using medication. This method is also great at helping relieve chronic pain because it helps you relax and take the focus off the pain. Progressive relaxation involves a simple two-step process. First, you tense the muscle group that you are working on and then you let the tension out by relaxing the muscles. You will then take notice of how the relaxed state feels which helps you relax easier the more you do this method. You can either begin at the bottom of your body and then you work up or you can begin at the top of your body and work your way down. Before you start, make sure that you are in a comfortable position lying down on your back. Then you can begin.

- With your first muscle group or body part, breathe in, and tense the first muscle group (Tense firmly, but not to the point of pain or cramping.) for about 4 to 10 seconds. Be mindful that you do not tense too hard and cause pain which defeats the purpose of the exercise

- Then breathe out and completely relax the muscle group as quickly as you can (do not relax it gradually).
- Keep the muscle group or body part in the relaxed state for about 10 to 20 seconds before you work on the next muscle group.
- Notice the difference between how the muscles feel when they are tense and how they feel when they are relaxed. The relaxed state is helpful to know so if you ever needed to relax without doing this body scan, your muscle memory can kick in.
- When you are finished with all of the muscle groups, count backward from 5 to 1 to bring your focus back to the present.

The great thing about this technique is you do not have to be tense in order to practice it. It is best to practice it when you are calm so when you are anxious you are able to go through the steps without being confused since you've already practiced it. The body map you can follow when doing the body scan can look like this. You can start on one side and do one side completely and then go to the other side of your body. You can also do both sides at the same time before progressing to the next side of your body. This example body scan goes from the bottom of your body to the top of your body, by doing one side at a time.

- Feet - Wiggle your toes and point them to your face. Then point your toes downward. If you feel any tension from the waist down when you do this, relax your body.
- Lower foot and leg - Make your calf muscles tense by pointing your toes towards you.
- Thighs - Squeeze them hard and then let them go.
- Entire leg - Squeeze your thighs again and note any tension you may experience. Release the tension.
- Glutes - Squeeze your butt together and then release them.
- Hips - Roll your hips around and then let them go.

- Stomach - Hold your stomach in and then let it go.
- Back - Arch your stomach away from where you are resting and then bring it back down.
- Chest - Take a very deep breath for 5 to 15 seconds.
- Hand - Close your fist as tightly as possible and then let it go.
- Upper arms and biceps - Squeeze your fingers into a fist, bend your arm at your elbow and then flex your bicep in the muscle formation.
- Forearms and wrists - Extend them and bend your hands back at your wrist.
- Shoulders - Perform a shrug. Try to bring your shoulders as high as possible, aim for your ear, and let the shrug go.
- Front of the neck - Move your chin downward and try not to cause tension in your head and neck when you do it.
- Back of the neck - Press your head into the floor as far back as possible.
- Your mouth and the area around your mouth - Purse your lips as tightly as possible.
- Jaws and cheeks - Smile the widest smile that you can.
- Around the bridge of your nose and eyes - Wiggle your nose and then close your eyes as tightly as possible.
- Forehead - Frown as deeply as possible and wrinkle your forehead while you do so.

Once you finish going to the top on one side and make it to your forehead, you can go back down throughout the rest of your body. Once you are great at practicing the entire body, you can make the exercise shorter by doing a shorter version that focuses on the main body parts. You can also pick and choose what body parts you would like to scan so you can create your own customized progressive scan. A shortened body scan example would look like this:

- Lower limbs (legs and feet) – Point your toes upward, tense your calves and squeeze your thighs on both sides.
- Stomach and chest – Breathe in and breathe out as deeply as possible and feel your stomach contract as far as possible.
- Shoulders, arms, neck – Raise your shoulders up high as possible and let them go. You can flex your biceps and then bend your wrists as far back as possible. Be sure to do this on both sides of your body.
- Face – Wrinkle your forehead and the area around your nose. Smile as widely as possible and frown as widely as possible to work your entire face.

After becoming a pro at knowing how your body feels when it is relaxed. You can then focus on the relaxed or released part only. You can do the full body by relaxing or the shortened body. Initially, the release only technique may feel different as it will feel less intense than the full tense and release exercise, but the more you practice, the more you feel comfortable with the full exercise.

Great job working through this chapter! Hopefully, you've made plenty of notes and highlighted the exercises you want to try. This chapter highlighted all the ways that you can use breathing and relaxation exercises to add to your mindfulness meditation practice. The breathing exercises draw from some popular yoga breathing exercises like lion's breath, *kumbhakam, ujjayi,* and bee breath, spirit of fire, and bellows breath to name a few. Some breathing exercises also include popular breathing techniques such as equal breathing, 4:7:8 breathing, and left and right nostril breathing. Popular relaxation methods covered in the chapter are autogenic relaxation, progressive relaxation, and visualization techniques. The next two chapters will focus on specific mindfulness meditation scripts that you can use to help you start your mindfulness meditations and to diversify your meditation practice.

Chapter 4: Mindfulness Meditation Exercises

"A mind set in its ways is wasted." – Eric Schmidt

When was the last time that you tried to learn something new? Maybe you had to try out a new recipe or take a new way to work? Perhaps you have to try a brand-new form of communication that was drastically different from what you have already tried when communicating. Whatever it is that you had to learn, I'm sure that it was not the easiest thing. However, once you finally learned what to do, how awesome was the feeling to know that you accomplished something? As you start off with meditating, it may be a little rocky at first, but keep going! You will learn how to get better. And that's when the real run begins.

So, it is time to take the fun up a notch. The next two chapters are dedicated to giving you guided mindfulness meditation exercises that you can practice on your own. Before you begin, do not forget to be in the most comfortable place possible in your meditation place. You can lie down, be in lotus pose, sit or stand up. If you are sitting, try to have your back and posture as straight as possible. If you are lying down, let your arms and hands rest loosely beside you without having any tension in them. You can also decide to have the lights on or lights off. You can also decide if you want to keep your eyes open, closed or half-open. It can be very relaxing while you meditate, so make sure that having your eyes closed will not cause you to go to sleep! Remember, breathing is at the core of your exercises. So as you listen, remember to breathe in and breathe out. If at any point, you feel that your concentration is beginning to shift, firmly and quickly bring your attention back to your breath and to the meditation script.

Basic Mindfulness Meditation (Short)

Before you begin, be in the most comfortable position for you. You can dim the lights or keep them on. You can open or close your eyes, whatever is most comfortable. As you begin, try to slide into a calm state by relaxing your thoughts. Inhale to three counts and then exhale for three counts. Imagine your body receiving the life force of oxygen bringing energy to every part of your body that your breath touches.

If your thoughts are speeding by, try to slow them down and just watch them as they pass. As you see each one of them pass by, put them in a box. Inhale deeply through your diaphragm and exhale through your mouth. Feel the breath tickle your throat as the tension is exhaled out.

Whatever is upsetting you or whatever is making you happy, release those thoughts from any judgment you may have. Observe them as they are without trying to fix your problems, looking for solutions or wishing the problems will go away. Watch your thoughts glide by in your mind until they are gone. Bring your attention back to your breath. Breathe in deeply and then breathe out through your mouth.

Be aware of what your mind is thinking but try not to focus in on them to the point that you are not breathing deeply. Remember to breathe in deeply from your diaphragm. Lengthen your shallow breathing with your deep breaths. Notice the calm that the deep breathing brings to your body. Breathe in through your nose for a count of five, 1, 2, 3, 4, 5, and let the breath out through your mouth for a count of five, 1, 2, 3, 4, 5. Feel the breath rippling through your body as you breathe in again. Then let the breath go back out.

When you breathe in through your nose this time, take in as much air as you can possibly manage. Feel the breath powering you and just be. Be still. Be in the moment. Embrace the physical sensations around you. If you're sitting on a fluffy rug, feel the rug. Feel the material of your clothes rub against your skin. Feel the arms on your hair tingle.

Inhale and feel your chest move gently up. Then exhale and feel your chest move down. Exhale until it feels like your back is touching the floor. Feel the power that deep breathing has on your entire body.

Inhale and exhale through your mouth. Make a gentle whoosh as the breath leaves your body. Stay calm and relaxed. If you find yourself losing focus, do not beat yourself up. Be gentle and kind to yourself. Bring your focus right back to your breathing. Breathe. Hold your breath for a count of 5 seconds. Exhale for a count of 5 seconds. And let that breath out for 3 seconds. When you breathe in, feel your entire body relaxing with the force of the breath that you breathe in.

Wiggle your fingers, your toes, your nose, and your eyes. Feel the skin wrinkle and smooth once you return your body back to its resting position. Inhale deeply and be in the moment. Exhale deeply and be in the moment.

Feel the presence of your being. Reward yourself for taking the time to be mindful. Be grateful that you have the chance to be still and take in this very moment, not the past, not the future, not one minute from now, just the very present moment. Breathe gently in and out. Do not feel like you have something else to do or you need to rush this moment. No. Indulge in the presence of yourself and the universe. You are a wonderful being that is able to fully appreciate this moment through your breath.

Your inhales and exhales anchor you to the present time and give your appreciation for being able to be still. Breathe in this time hold your inhale for at least 10 seconds. Let go and exhale for another 5 Seconds. If you are not able to inhale for at least 10 seconds, that's okay. Inhale for as much as you can. Exhale.

Center your focus back on the moment and prepare yourself to bring yourself back to your critical mind. Prepare your moment for embracing the present time and every second that it brings, whether good or bad. Open your eyes and welcome the light. Try to keep this state of mindfulness as you move throughout the intensity of the day.

Basic Mindfulness Meditation (Long)

Find the most comfortable spot for your body to rest, whether that is lying down, standing up, or sitting. If you have on any tight clothes, loosen them so your body can feel free and unrestricted. You can turn off the lights in your room or close your eyes. If you are at risk of going to sleep, keep your eyes half-closed.

Breathe in and then exhale. Shed any judgment that you may have on thoughts that are passing by. Instead of thinking of your thoughts as criminals that must stand before you, the judge, do not mete out any punishment for the thoughts that you think. Merely let them skate by like a pair of young kids on roller skates. Inhale and use your deep breaths to steadily slow those thoughts down. The more air you take in the slower those breaths are.

Exhale all the tension out of your body for a count of four, 1, 2, 3 and 4. Then hold your breath for 7 seconds. 1, 2, 3, 4, 5, 6, and 7. Then breathe in for a count of 8: 1, 2, 3, 4, 5, 6, 7 and 8. Wonderful.

Breathe in deeply until you feel your heart rate slow. Breathe out deeply until you feel your heartbeat at a steady pace. Notice the thoughts that you feel. And let them be. You just be, as well. Let only your breathing connect your body to this present moment in time. Do not think about tomorrow. Do not think about what you're going to do after this recording. Do not think about what you did before this recording. Focus only on your breathing and being still.

If it is easier for you, exhale and open your mouth wildly. Exhale all of your expectations and items on your to-do list. Exhale all the anxiety and unpleasantness you may feel. When you inhale, breathe and feel the pleasure of just being. Feel the calmness taking over your body. Breathe in the importance of being able to be still and know that everything is going to be okay. Feel any tingling or sensations you may have. If you feel numb, or any discomfort, slightly shift your body until you are comfortable again.

Then close your eyes, and if you feel the flutter of your eyes against your eyelids, be grateful for that. Know that your body is simply floating in this moment in time. Instead of trying to anchor your body with heavy thoughts, let it simply be. You and your body are perfect as is. Reward yourself for being mindful by taking in a deep gulp of air. Then let out all the heavy burdens that are weighing you down through your breath. Breathe in again.

Imagine that relaxation is wrapping your entire body like a magical carpet. Your deep inhales power the carpet, and your deep exhales keep the carpet floating. If you find that your mind is wandering, bring those thoughts back to focus by focusing on your breath. Do not judge yourself if you're having trouble focusing initially. Commend yourself for trying. Remember you will continue to get better with time. Always bring the attention back to your breath.

Slightly feel the 'whoosh' of the breath leaving your nostrils and tickling your nose hairs. Welcome that breath back into your body by breathing deep from within the walls of your stomach. Feel that breath traveling through your stomach, up to your chest, up to your head, and returning back down, straight down to your feet. Exhale and breathe in and then feel the breath travel throughout every bone in your spine and throughout every finger back through your mouth.

Do that one more time. Take a deep breath from the pit of your diaphragm. Then exhale the air back out into the world just as deeply as you took the breath in. Great job.

Breathe in deeply and feel the breath traveling throughout every orifice of your body giving you energy, confidence, and gratefulness for being able to reflect on this moment. When you exhale, exhale those intentions good or bad that you are having. Do not feel the need to be industrious. Do not feel the need to be so awful to yourself.

Enjoy this moment to refresh by concentrating on your breathing. Take another deep breath and hold it for as long as you can. Exhale that breath for as long as you can. Breathing one more time and then open your eyes.

Wiggle your fingers and toes. Feel the force of energy move into your wrists and back into your hands. On the count of three open your eyes: 1, 2, 3.

Take the mindfulness with you throughout every moment of your day. Know that anytime you need to be mindful, you are armed with a tool that can help you remain calm and happy and mindful by using your breath. Feel free to use this tool at any time throughout your day.

Breathing Meditation (Short)

For this breathing meditation, we will focus on your breathing. This 5-minute breathing exercise is perfect for those on the go. This exercise is intended to help you focus on your breathing while replenishing your body with the energizing mentally clarifying power of your breath. You can lie down or stand up or sit whatever is most comfortable for you. Before you begin, make sure that you are in a comfortable position with the lights dimmed. Feel loose by tensing your fingers and your toes and letting them go. Do that one more time.

Point your toes as far as they can to your head. Then relax your toes and let your toes go back to a comfortable position.

Now that you're in your comfortable position, take one deep breath in. Feel your stomach draw in like it is touching your spine. Feel your stomach get as flat as possible. Lift your head up and breathe out. Breathe out all the bad thoughts and negativity that may be pent up. Feel the power of the breath circulating throughout your body. Feel the air touch every part of your body and bringing energy and positive vibes.

For the next breath sequence, we're going to try a lion's breath. Gently make sure that your hands are lying to your side of your body. Let them stay there resting without feeling like you have to move them. If they are clenched, unclench them and let them feel loose. Feel the calmness of your hands and let that feeling transpose on to your body. This time when you breathe in, breathe in as deeply as you can. Breathe in with your mouth closed. Then open your mouth and let the breath out like a lion roar. It is okay to make a loud sound. Stick your tongue out to get all of the air out of your esophagus. Close your mouth.

For this breath sequence, do a seven-count inhale. Breathe in for 7 seconds: 1, 2, 3, 4, 5, 6, 7. Then exhale for eight counts: 1, 2, 3, 4, 5, 6, 7, 8. What a wonderful deep and full breath sequence. Feel how calm and smooth and relaxed your entire body feels. Feel how light your body feels. Breathe in again.

There are no thoughts about today, tomorrow, or even the future that is bogging you down. Relish this lightness. Remember this feeling of relaxation. Let's try another deep 4:7:8 breath sequence. Making sure that you are breathing deeply, place your hand on your stomach and breathe in deeply. Feel your hand draw back as close to your body as your stomach is drawing in as much breath as you can. Exhale for 4 seconds: 1, 2, 3, 4. Hold your breath for seven seconds. Then imagine you are a gas tank. Take as much air in as possible. then hold your breath for 7 seconds: 1, 2, 3, 4, 5, 6, 7.

Now just like air is coming out the balloon, open your mouth and exhale all of that air out. Feel the relaxed feeling that's rocking your body. Feel how good it feels. Be aware of your breath only. Imagine that when you are just being, you radiate a beautiful color. It can be your favorite color. The more you are being and the calmer you are, the more vibrant your body radiates.

Breathe in deeply again and exhale just as deeply again. We will be ending the meditation soon so gently stir your mindful mind.

Slightly come back to this moment of critical awareness. When you get back to your critical mind, feel the necessity to be mindful throughout the rest of your day.

On the count of three, open your eyes and gently lift up. You can slowly stand and pack yourself on the back for completing a great breathing exercise. One. Two. Three.

Awareness of Breath Practice

For this exercise, awareness of your breath is the object. Please begin by feeling comfortable in a safe special place. Be in a dignified position whether that is lying down, sitting down, or in Lotus Pose. Just for a few moments, give way to your breathing and feel your breath coursing throughout your entire body. Replace all the tension and anxiety and shallow breathing in your body, with total complete relaxation and deep breathing. Feel your body responding to the deep breaths. Feel how your heartbeat slows. Notice how the tension removes from your body with every breath. Once you are there, imagine what your relaxed body feels like. Feel your body going limp like a noodle but not a soggy noodle, and al dente noodle. Feel soft and relaxed, yet firm. Hang loose and comfortable. Let all the tension leave your body.

Allow your breaths to rule the moment. In this present moment, you want to let your thoughts wander delicately around your brain. Let them bounce gently around the walls of your mind. Instead of your thoughts bouncing quickly and rapidly, let them bounce smoothly and steadily. Observe what the thoughts are. Once you observe the thought, imagine that they disappear with a soft poof. Let the thoughts leave and just be. Still your brain again.

In the meantime, give all the attention to your breath. You want to breathe in deeply through your nose. Feel the breath enter your nostrils and down your throat. When you exhale, exhale through your mouth and feel the breath leave your tongue and your teeth and makes it back into the world outside of you. Feel what your body feels like when it is just still. Your body is warm and empty and open. With every breath that you feel, imagine the oxygen in your bloodstream sending energy to every part of your body.

When you inhale notice how freeing it feels. Notice how the oxygen replaces any negativity that may be in your body. Instead of focusing on negative thoughts, have no judgment. Your thoughts are just that. If you're having positive thoughts, have no judgment on those thoughts. Just let them be. Focus on the breath Breathe in gently but deeply and exhale just as deeply. If you want to make a soft sound with your inhales and your exhales, that's fine. If you would like to try a huge lion's breath at this time, feel free to do so. Take a deep breath in and then exhale the breath out. When you exhale, let yourself exhale with an audible 'aah' like your own personal roar.

Feel how empowering that feels. Feel how wonderful it is to let out all of your anxiety in tension in your personal lion roar. Try it one more time.

Breathe in for a count of five: 1, 2, 3, 4, 5. Then let out your personal roar one more time for the count of five: 1, 2, 3, 4, 5. Stick your tongue out this time when you exhale. Feel your heartbeat, and calm it down by taking in one huge breath. Then you can let it out. Breathe in and feel how your body reacts. Breathe out and feel how your body reacts. Notice how your body feels between each breath.

Next, we are going to try a bellows breath. This will speed up your heart rate and then we will slow it back down.

Breathe in. Breathe out. Make each breath that you breathe in the same length and depth as the breath that you breathe out. We will do this four more times.

Breathe in. Breathe out. Hold your breath for three counts. One. Two. Three.

Breathe in deeply from your diaphragm, then breathe out for the same count length until your stomach is as flat as it can be. Great job.

If you feel distracted at all, move the thought to the side. Let it disappear and bring your attention and focus back to your breath. We have two more bellow breaths.

Inhale. Then exhale.

Breathe in and breathe out. Hold the breath. Good job. Now breathe deeply and smoothly. Feel how awesome our breathing is. What a wonderful tool is it. See how wonderful is can change our heartbeats or moods with the simple sustenance of air and good breathing.

The breaths are bolstering your present breath. If you're comfortable in your position, think of a nice gentle breeze blowing right over your body. Feel comfortable being in this moment. You do not have to think about the worries of today, tomorrow, or the future. You're simply feeling comfortable and still. See the clouds floating above in the sky. Look at all the delightful shapes they are making, gradually, smoothly, and changing.

Whatever thoughts you're having that may make you lose focus, gently wipe them to the side. Hear the wash of the waves against the shore relaxing your body. Imagine the warm temperature rocking you to a state of relaxation. Feel at peace with the noise of fun around you on each side of the beach. See a small crab walking by your beach chair. Stay calm and watch it pass. Instead of holding your breath, breathe in deeply and slowly until the crab passes. Enjoy the warmth of the sun warming you.

Relax your body to the point that you feel like you're about to enter a deep sleep, but you're aware of everything around you. Feel the breath tugging your throat as you breathe gently and fully. Feel your lungs expanding. Taking as much breath as you can. Hold it there. Let the breast bubble out and give power all throughout your body. Breathe out make a slight 'O' with your mouth until all the breath is out. Feel like a balloon with no air left in it.

Once your breath is out, inhale again and gently awaken your senses. Feel your body arriving back into your critical space. You can slowly turn the switch back on to the grind, but this time, instead of moving so fast, take a step a little bit slower. Be a little bit more mindful when you are doing your usual activities in your day to day living. We will bring the meditation to a close soon. However, do not feel any pressure to end soon. If you would like to continue being mindful for a few more moments, that's ok. When you are ready to end the meditation, you can gently open your eyes.

Once your eyes are open, you can stand and have a wonderful day. Take the state of relaxation with you throughout the rest of your day.

Breathscape Practice

For this session, you will be guided through a meditation session that uses your breath as is the main focus of awareness. Before we begin, please spend time fixing your body in a comfortable position. If you are sitting, try to keep your spine as straight as possible, stick your check out, and have your head up. Let your head be balanced squarely between your shoulders, and let your gaze rest softly and gently as a point in space or a point on the wall. If it is more comfortable, you can close your eyes. Allow your hands and arms to rest in the position that is most comfortable for you. Do not let them feel heavy. Let them feel loose and light.

Before we go any further, turn off the switch to your daily grind. For the next few moments, no thinking about what types of things you need to do. No thinking of what someone said to you that pissed you off. No thinking of what you didn't get done to do. Please turn on the switch to your mindfulness mode. You are allowing yourself to stop for a moment and delight in this mindfulness. This switch only allows you to focus on what's going on in the present moment. Your mindfulness switch is only kind to your thoughts. You are no longer judgmental of what you think. You are only watching the thoughts as they go by. Now you are only aware of what's happening in this present moment. As you sit in a comfortable position, be still and feel. Feel the small hum of your breath as your chest moves up and down. Enjoy all the physical sensations that come with just being. Imagine that you are the epitome of what it means to be a bump on a log.

Be aware of how your stomach moves while breathing and exhaling. Feel how the air travels through your nostrils and then feel the slight lift of your shoulders and in your chest. Observe your breath cycle especially where it feels the strongest. When you feel that you are getting the most air, how does it feel? At one point do you feel like you are getting the most air? Is it when your stomach is drawn in as you feel your chest with air, or does your breath cycle feel the strongest when the breath comes in through your nostrils? Travel with your breath from when it comes through your nose, goes to your lungs, and pushes out your stomach slightly. Feel how the breath goes out of your body.

Observe the in-between movement of your breath. Notice the in-between time of when your breath comes in and when your breath goes out. Think of the entire sequence of breathing in and breathing out as one complete breath cycle. Notice how every part of your breath cycle is special, and it helps bring life into you. Focus on the moment in between your breath cycles. Try to even it out and make it the same depth, length and intensity as your inhales and exhale.

Inhale. Exhale. Space in between. Inhale. Exhale. Space in between.

While you focus on your breaths, you may experience your mind traveling. You may think about what happened last night or what you need to do after this or what you did before this session or something that's bothering you. Allow those thoughts to sashay right out of your mind. Bring your attention back to your breaths as gently as possible. Feel your breath and the sensations it provides as it travels throughout your body. Be aware of how your mind can easily go from one thing to one thing and bring it back to focus on your breathing. I know you may want to control your breathing at this time, but relinquish control and let your breath flood your chest cavity.

Imagine that you are in a field of flowers. You're rolling in a meadow and enjoying the soft carpet of greenery. The vivid colors embrace you and cause you to go to your happy place. Do not feel the need to control what time you have to leave from the field. Stay in the field and breathe in and breathe out. Smell the sweet scents floating in the field.

As you are in the field, you may hear background sounds. You may hear the movement of traffic, of cars coming and going. You may also hear the hum of a heating and cooling unit or people moving in the background. Focus on the sound itself briefly, then bring your focus back to your breath. You're connected to those sounds through your breath. You are connected to this Moment by your breathing. Every time you're focused, but get off track, kindly bring it back. While you're focusing on your breath, notice how you may feel the need to have an opinion on this moment.

Maybe you like my voice, maybe you do not, maybe you do not like the position that you're sitting in. Be aware of this tendency to feel like you have to notice what's going on and have an opinion about it. Instead of focusing on the decision to have an opinion, let the need for that go. Throw your opinion away and just be. Focus on the situation as it is. It is not good or bad it is just is. Notice that the only thing that you are focusing on at this time is your breath and the physical sensations that come with your breath cycle.

At this point, you may be feeling slightly uncomfortable, or you're ready to stop. You can deal with the sensations by slowly moving your feet so they do not go to sleep or slightly to appease the discomfort. This may be one way to do with it. Another way to deal with your physical discomfort is to just experience it a little while longer. Allow your discomfort to go one more moment and see what it feels like. Do you feel any tingling or numbness? Embrace it. It will soon pass. You can deal with it, just experience whatever you are feeling right now fully. There is not one better way more than the other.

Notice your intentions at this moment. Remove the intentions and just be. On your next breath, lose your intentions. Focus only on your breath. Breathe in and then breathe out. Notice how everything comes back to your breath. Now if you have gone way off into left field, that's totally okay. Use your breath to bring back attention to your breath.

Embrace the power of your cycle of breathing. Notice how the breath can help you ride the good thoughts and bad thoughts. See that when even you go off to be distracted, you can focus on your breathing and bring it back to just being in the moment without having to make any decision.

Be proud of yourself for noticing that you have gotten off track but you're able to get back into focus with your breath. Great job on being mindful. Keep that thought of mindfulness with you and the importance of breathing as you go along your way.

Now that the meditation is coming to an end, feel proud that you were able to spend this time building your muscle of awareness by breathing. Be grateful that you have been able to spend this time in this present moment and transfer this skill to other moments in your life. Be grateful that you are able to walk day-by-day in the present moment without being judgmental.

Mindfulness Meditation for Relaxation and Stress Relief

Before we begin this meditation, take a few moments to get comfortable and loose. It is now time to turn your mind off from the busy hustle and bustle of everyday grind and just focus on being in the moment. This meditation is to help you be present and relax and relieve any stress that may be penned up.

We will start with a few deep breaths from the depth of your abdomen. Breathe in through your nose and then blow the air out your mouth. Every time you breathe, feel your stomach come as close to your insides as possible and when you breathe out, let out an audible 'aah.' Does your breathing focus on the physical sensations that come with that deep breaths? This time when you inhale open your mouth and breathe through your mouth. Feel the air tickle your teeth on your tongue. Feel your lungs fill with the great life force of air. During this time, put all your troubles to the side. Breathe them out with every exhale that you take.

You no longer need to feel shackled by any pressure you may be feeling. Try to calm your thoughts from racing. Just observe your thoughts as they go by. Do you notice any thoughts that seem to be re-occurring? Do you notice any patterns from the things that you are thinking? Breathe in and let the thoughts go to the side. Breathe in and breathe out.

When you inhale, feel every part of your body that the air touches relaxing. The deeper you inhale, the more you feel relaxed. Every time you exhale, let the tension escape your body.

Start at your feet. Breathe in and stretch the breath upward. When you breathe, feel the breath relaxing your feet and toes. Feel the air melt in your attention like ice. Breathe in and let your legs, hips, and waist relax. Feel the tension liquify like ice. Next move up to your stomach. Feel the inhale spread the walls of your abdomen. Breathe out and feel the tension in your chest melt away when you exhale. Mentally tell yourself to relax.

Feel your chest filled with air. Feel your entire body dripping with air and feel the warmth in your chest when you exhale. Now, work your way up to your neck. Feel the warmth of the air and warm up your entire neck. Feel the tension leave your neck. You can now breathe in and feel the warmth feel your entire head. Draw I your breath deeply, and then feel yourself relax. Feel your entire body relax as you exhale that breath out.

Be in the moment. Feel calm and be ok with that. Be completely still. Tune out any background noises that you may be hearing. Do not focus on those noises. Focus on your breath. To focus even more, focus on your heartbeat. Notice how it changes with your breath. The deeper your breaths are, the slower your heartbeat is. The faster your breaths are, the faster your heartbeat goes. Keep your breaths, slow and deep.

Do you notice any spots of tension in your body? Breathe in and feel the tension go away with every breath. Bring your head down to your chest and bring it back up. Then push your head back as far as it can go. Stop and enjoy the release. Squeeze your eyes tight and then loosen them. Wrinkle your nose and the area around your bridge. Let the tension go away with every wriggle. Then wiggle your forehead. Then let the tension melt away with every forehead wiggle.

Breathe in and let the tension in your eyes go away again. Shrug your shoulders up. Keep them up and let them go down. Then breathe in and with your breath, let them out slowly. Bring awareness to your arms. Breathe in and then let the arms move upward with your breath and let them go. Move to your wrists and move them back and forth. Stop and then feel the looseness of your wrists.

You should now feel your body in a total state of deep relaxation. Now go back to your thighs. Imagine them being completely relaxed now. Feel your entire body relax. Breathe in and inhale for four counts: 1, 2, 3, 4. Let out your breath before for four counts: 1, 2, 3, 4. The meditation will be coming to an end soon. Slowly open your eyes.

Blink and welcome the day. Now you can stand up and move forward. Keep the feeling of relaxation and stress-free feeling with you as you go about your day-to-day tasks.

Mindfulness Meditation for Inner Peace and Calm

Find a comfortable position by sitting or lying down and close your eyes. This meditation is to help you find inner peace and calm. We will begin by noticing your breath. Please breathe in through your nose and exhale through your mouth.

With every breath, feel the coolness of the air touching every organ with peace as it feels your lungs. Feel your lungs with a breast as deep as you can hold. With every breath, feel the power of your breath and the reinvigoration it brings. With every breath, bring stillness, hope, and peace to your busy mind.

Throughout the meditation, your mind may begin to wonder and focus on different types of things. Gently and firmly guide your thoughts back to your breaths. As you inhale, fuel your body with breath. Feel the breath charging your body and preparing you for whatever comes ahead.

As you exhale, rid itself of any fresh negativity or bad germs that are over your body. With each breath, feel your body being replenished with peace and calm until no more negativity is left. Focus on your breath for 10 counts and then let go.

Breathe in and breathe out. Feel the warmth of your body with every breath. Feel the gentle feeling of lightness that spreads through your body with every single breath that you take.

When you inhale with this breath, repeat, 'I am peaceful.' Think of what brings peace to you. Repeat, 'I am peaceful.'

Exhale and feel negativity being scooped out your body in a pile to the side that you can discard. Do not worry about the negativity. Negativity is the least of your concerns. You are concerned about your breathing and the power of a single breath.

Breathe in and feel relaxed. State to yourself, 'I am calm.' What brings your calmness. Experience a double dose of that calmness by thinking of an image that brings your calm. Think about this image as you continue to inhale and exhale.

With every breath, feel your extremities relax and loosen the tension within until you feel better. Do not feel discouraged if you are not feeling as relaxed as you need to be. Continue to focus on your breathing.

Breathe out slowly and completely. Notice the slight space between every breath cycle. Breathe in and then let your body feel every single ray of relaxation like the sun spreading all over your body.

Breathe in, and repeat, 'I am calm. No matter what.' Do not think of any circumstances that can change your mood, whether those circumstances are good or bad. Focus rather on being calm regardless of the circumstances surrounding you no matter what situation you may find yourself in.

Breathe out and then breathe back in. Feel that you are calm no matter what. Breathe out. Breathe in and feel the breath bringing calmness to you. It anchors you and brings you peace with any situation that you may encounter.

Repeat to yourself, 'I am at peace. No matter what.' Keep this in mind that whatever may be bothering you, feel calm no matter what. Keep the spirit of calmness within you and take it with you as you go.

As we bring this meditation to a close, keep this feeling of peaceful calm centered within you and let it carry you throughout the day. Feel empowered to be present and mindful for a few more moments if you choose to do so. The benefits of mindfulness do not have to be rushed. Take your time and do as you please.

Whenever you are ready, we will end the meditation on the count of five: 1, 2, 3, 4, 5.

<u>Mindfulness meditation for self-compassion</u>
Let's begin by getting in a comfortable and dignified position. You can sit, be in lotus pose, or lie down. Then take in three deep breaths.

Breathe in. Feel the oxygen relax in your entire body. Breathe out. Push the air out as far as you can.

Inhale. Feel like you're sucking in a straw and draw as much as in as possible. Count to four counts: 1, 2, 3, 4. Exhale for four counts: 1, 2, 3, 4. You can let your imaginary straw go.

Inhale one more time. Four counts: 1, 2, 3, 4. Exhale for four counts: 1, 2, 3, 4.

Again, make sure that you are in the most comfortable position possible and switch your focus to the breathing. This meditation is all about being compassionate with yourself. Too many times, we can be our harshest critic. Too many times we can fall victim to trying to comparing ourselves with others. This meditation seeks to disrupt that train of thought. This meditation is all about being compassionate to yourself according to the place that you are at this very moment. Not at the place you were yesterday or will be in the future, but this meditation is all about being grateful for the person that you are at this very moment.

Focus on your breath and be aware of the words that we will be saying. Let the words fill your body space in the same way your breath anchors you. Try and feel the power of your words and the power of your breath at the same time.

If you have any pressing thoughts or any worrisome thoughts that are bothering you like a gnat in the background, swat them away. But if they come back just allow them to be. Make note of those thoughts and bring your attention back to your breath.

Feel where the breath is most obvious to you. Feel it deeply as the breath travels up your nose throughout the rest of your body. When you exhale, feel your breath when it is leaving your body. Feel it taking all of the toxins and negativity of your environment away with it.

Whatever you feel that breath is doing, focus on the sensation of breathing and what your breath cycle looks like. With every inhale, take the nurturing warmth of your breath and let it spread throughout your body just like a pond ripple in your favorite lake.

With every exhale, say, "I am happy." Think of what makes you happy. Think of what delights you. Think of how your body feels when you are in your happy place. Repeat to yourself that "I am happy."

Breathe in and exhale say, "I am safe." Know that you are safe no matter what you may do. Know that you are safe right now as you are mindful. Know that your thoughts are safe. You are in a judgment-free zone. There are no good thoughts or bad thoughts. They are just thoughts.

Breathe in and breathe out. Say, "I am kind to myself." Whatever mistakes you have made in the past, they are gone. Learn from them.

Whatever evil, malicious things you have done, they are gone. Say it again, "I am kind to myself." Breathe in and exhale again.

Breathe in and breathe out. Repeat to yourself, "I accept myself for who I am today." Breathe in. And breathe out. You are perfect. Your perfections and imperfections make you the perfect you. Breathe in and breathe out, and say, "I accept myself for who I am today."

Inhale and exhale. Say "I forgive myself." Guess what? Whatever has been done has been done. Forgive yourself from the nice you and mean you. Be gentle, but firm. Learn what you need from every situation. It is there for your reflection and understanding. Breathe in and breathe out. Say, "I forgive myself."

Breathe in. Breathe out, and say, "I am healthy." If you can breathe, you are able to be healthy. If you are breathing, you can always improve your health. Be still in the moment and think of how you can improve your health. If you are already healthy, encourage yourself to stay on the healthy path. Breathe in and breathe out. Say, "I am healthy."

Breathe in. Breathe out. And say, "I practice self-compassion daily." Feel how compassionate you feel for yourself. Know that you are free from judgment. Feel free from harsh judgments of yourself. Feel free from being upset about any mistakes that you have made. Breathe in and breathe out. Repeat again, "I practice self-compassion daily."

Breathe in and breathe out. Feel free to make use of the phrases in whichever order you would like. You can either rest and continue to breathe in and breathe out. Or you can repeat your favorite affirmation.

Whichever you decide, that is fine. There is no right or wrong answer. Do what is most comfortable for you. Whatever you decide, try to be mindful of your decision.

The meditation will be coming to an end soon. Do what you must. If you are enjoying this exercise, and you want to take the time to continue to be mindful, you are able to do that. If you must get up to continue about your day, you can do that as well.

When it's time, slightly awaken your senses and return to the critical mind on the count of three. One. Two. Three.

Open your eyes and be fortified by your self-compassion meditation.

In conclusion, the guided meditations in this chapter can help you get started. They are especially helpful if you are not sure how to begin or what to say if you want to be mindful. These meditations are great to practice the different ways that you can breathe and improve the ways that you can be mindful. Now we will move to a few guided meditations that affect specific sicknesses in the next chapter.

Chapter 5: Healing Mindfulness Meditation Exercises

"If you are facing in the right direction, all you need to do is keep on walking." – Buddha

Buddha said it well. Now that you are walking in the right direction of doing your own guided meditations, it is now time for you to keep on walking and learning. The mindfulness meditation exercises in this chapter are going to focus on healing and coping with anxiety, depression, insomnia, and grief. Research has shown that mindfulness meditation is quite beneficial in helping you heal these illnesses due to the boost in mental and heart health. Mindfulness meditation is also a great tool to help with coping with these types of challenges because it also draws on your inner strength and the power of the breath. The following guided mindfulness meditation exercises will help you to relax and cope with the illnesses that you may be dealing with.

Mindfulness Meditation for Anxiety

We will begin our mindfulness meditation for anxiety right now. If you are experiencing anxiety currently or have been experiencing it for a while, I know it is not the best feeling in the world. You may be hurting. You may be scared, but know that you're going to be okay. I know it is hard for you to believe this right now, but know that the responses your body is giving to your anxiety are going to be over soon.

Know that relief from your anxiety is coming. It does not last forever. Do you want to know why? It is because your body has a built-in stress relief already. Your body will naturally deal with anxiety on its own terms. So keep this gem in the back of your mind and know that your body is always helping you deal with your anxiety. It is up to you to activate the stress-relief by being relaxed. It is up to you to help your body relax by taking in deep breaths. The inhales are going to help calm your body. The purpose of this meditation is to use your breathing in order to relax.

You may feel like it is difficult to breathe but be aware that your body is already breathing. Listen to your breath right now. If your breaths are short, try to lengthen your breath by breathing to the count of three. Breathe in for a cycle of three counts; 1, 2, 3. Then breathe out for a breath cycle of three: 1, 2, 3. Notice your heartbeat. Notice if it is going fast or slow.

Let's try to slow your breathing down. Breathe in again. This time we are going to hold the breath cycle for 5 counts. Breathe in: 1, 2, 3, 4, 5. Then breathe out: 1, 2, 3, 4, 5.

Breathe in deeply again. Now breathe out like you're blowing a birthday cake with a lot of candles. You want to make sure that you are blowing each and every one of those candles out. Breathe in and hold your breath in for three counts: 1, 2, 3. Now breathe out slowly: 1, 2, 3. Keep this up. You're doing a great job.

For extra support, you can hold up your fingers and pretend they are the candles in front of you. Now blow the air out open your mouth and make a slight sound as you blow it out. Make a gentle 'hoo' sounds as you let your breath out. You can do this breath cycle one more time, or you can continue to breathe slowly and gently.

Be aware of your body. See how your body is controlling your breathing? Do you see how your body makes sure that your body is getting enough air? Do you see how your body wants to help you calm down? In your comfortable position, close your eyes again and take it all in. Take in how awesome and self-sufficient your body is and how you can help it.

You may still feel overwhelmed. You may feel like no one is with you right now, but know that you are enough. You are your breathing. Your breath is a wave. With every deep inhale you give, the higher the wave is. Ride the wave as high as you can. Breathe in and let your breath out with a big whoosh.

If you want to feel more comfortable, feel free to turn the light off or stand up and pace around as you continue with these breathing exercises. If these steps do not help, know that your anxiety will continue to decrease on its own. You can continue to help your anxiety decrease by breathing. The more you breathe, the calmer you will be. Take it slow. Imagine with that feeling of calm feels like. Is it blue or yellow or white? Is it vivid, pastel, or bold? Feel that the deeper you breathe, the more you relax and the faster your anxiety will go.

As you breathe, feel that they are helping your body relax. With each breath, you breathe in, breathe in deeply and feel your body getting calmer. Please try and focus on your breath right now.

You do not have to worry about what is triggering you or causing you anxiety. You do not have to worry about what you're going to do to deal with the anxiety. The only thing you should focus on is your breathing. Feel the flutter of the clothing against your chest every time you breathe in and breathe out. If you're feeling uncomfortable, and you need to find a more comfortable position do so gently but continue to focus on your breath.

You are going to be okay. I know it doesn't feel like it, but you are going to be okay. Now we want to feel the warmth that's associated with calm. You can warm your hands together gently until you feel your palm slightly warming up. Do not go vigorously - go smoothly, slowly, and gently. Do you feel the warmth?

Now that you can focus on your hands moving, how does it sound? That sound can help you ground yourself from your anxiety and sent to you along with your breathing. When you feel that you focused on your hands enough, you can stop and place your hands by your side and breathe in again.

Relax and know that anxiety is normal. Focus on the sensations of your body. Notice how they're different from when you first began. Listen to the sound your breath makes as you breathe in and you breathe out. Moment by moment, the breath is helping you pass this level of anxiety.

Anxiety is a natural process. It is not always easy to feel, but it is natural. Help your body react by continuing to breathe. Do not have any judgment about your state of mind right now. Know that life happens. But when you're able to be in this moment, just like now, with your breath, you can focus on the good. You can focus on just being. You do not have to make a decision to do anything. Just be here right now with your breath and your body. Know that you're going to be okay.

Accept your body for what it is. Accept your brain for what it gives you. Accept your responses for what they are because they are what they are. affirmations to help you and your body recover. You can either listen and continue to breathe slowly or you can repeat them after with every breath.

Breathe in, and then breathe out. Repeat after me. "I accept who I am no matter what I am feeling." The past does not determine who I am, nor the future. The only thing that matters is the right now and by accepting who you are now, you are being mindful.

Breathe in, and then breathe out. Repeat after me. "I know that anxiety does not last forever. My anxiety will pass." Anxiety feels like it will last forever, but if you take it in the present moment, you will be able to ride the wave to calmness.

Breathe in, and then breathe out. Repeat after me. "My body is prepared to handle my anxiety. I can help by breathing." Be grateful and know that your body can handle any stress that it faces. The most important thing is to help your body out by breathing deeply.

Know that deep down inside, that as each second goes by and as every minute goes by, I feel my anxiety going away. And I feel a large dose of calm replacing it.

Repeat after me. "I feel relaxed. I am more comfortable." As you continue to breathe, notice how the breath is affecting your body.

Breathe in, and then breathe out. Repeat after me. "I accept how I feel right now. I am calm. I'm going to be okay. I am relaxed. I am at peace." Keep breathing. You will continue to feel your body come down from the anxiety that you are experiencing. Pay careful attention to how your body feels in the relaxed state.

Great job. Notice how you feel. Continue to feel relaxed. Continue to breathe in and breathe out. Notice how loose your limbs feel. Notice how easy your breaths come and go. Notice how easy it is for your body to pick up on the next breath after your first one.

Continue to relax for as long as you want. You can continue to stay in your comfortable position and breathe in and breathe out, or you can go ahead and bring the meditation to an end. Whatever you feel like doing, be mindful of the decision.

On the count of three, this meditation will be ending. You can replay this guided meditation again if you need to or continue to breathe deeply and silently on your own. One. Two. Three.

Mindfulness Meditation for Depression

In this meditation, we're going to focus on dealing with depression. Depression can sometimes feel like wearing sopping wet clothes. You want to dry them because you're wearing them, but it is the only pair you have. So you have to wear them wet, which can take a while. If you had a dryer you would put the clothes in there, but you do not, alas you have to let the clothes air-dry. This meditation will help the clothes dry smoother. I want to commend you for taking action for taking the first step of deciding to meditate.

For this meditation, start by being comfortable. You can be in a nice warm place where you won't be disturbed. We will need time for peace and quiet. We're going to start off breathing deeply for my diaphragm and releasing those breaths from our mouth. As we're breathing, switch out the cloud of doom and gloom above you to a cloud of white positive energy right above us. That energy is right over us. Wherever you go, you are able to get energy and positivity from it that can help make you stronger throughout the day. Every time you breathe in, that energy source gets stronger. Every time you breathe out, negativity, fear, anxiety your worries, and your depression gets weaker. The more you breathe, the stronger, your energy source will be.

Now let's imagine that we are at a beautiful lake house. You are in the middle of the forest with beautiful trees around and it smells like pine. The tall trees reach the sky and are tall and shady. You hang under the trees, and it is only you and your cloud of energy. Feel the beautiful, gentle breeze that goes across the lake while you're sending. Breathe in and feel the power level raise up. Feel calm feel at peace.

Now you want to dip your feet into the lake. Do so. You are floating in the middle of the water on a raft. Float on your back and make a ripple in the water with your finger. While you float on your back, you feel that cloud in the warm sunshine giving you energy. You have no room for the depression. It is going smaller. The more you laugh and giggle and enjoy yourself in the water the more it goes away.

While you were at your favorite place on the lake, think of some of your favorite sounds besides the water. What about the laugh of your baby? The giggle of a sibling or relative? The beautiful sound of fresh water dripping on the pine needles. The more you think of beautiful images as you breathe in, the more that cloud gets powered, your depression weakens and the clothes dry. Breathe in and breathe out. With every breath, feel how much dryer your clothes are beginning to feel.

At this time, just enjoy being in this moment. Feel how your body is beginning to relax. You feel so good, warm and relaxed. You could just go to sleep on the water, but you're not going to. Now you're going to stand upon your raft. Feel the sun on you trying out your body, but feel how reinvigorated you are.

Now as you bring yourself back to your body in your critical brain, you're going to breathe in that feeling of peaceful calm and serenity. Carry the feeling with you throughout the day. And then exhale. When you do so, exhale out any negative thoughts and feelings you may have.

Whenever you feel like your body is just soaking wet in soggy clothes, think about this wonderful energy source or your beautiful day at the beach and your lovely energy cloud that can dry you right out. You are able to feel the calmness from your breathing.

With every breath you take, imagine your white, warm ball of energy that is floating above you, replacing your tears with laughs. Imagine that warm cloud of energy replacing every negative thought you have with a positive one. Imagine that warm ball of energy arming you with calmness, strength, and positivity to right any depressive bout you may face.

Imagine the future where depression is no longer an issue for you. What does that day look like where you say goodbye to depression? What will you be wearing? What type of perfume or cologne will you wear? What will be your celebratory dinner? Are you going to celebrate with friends or by yourself?

Breathe in and then breathe out again. Call your awareness to this very moment. Enjoy the quiet calm joy that your breathing brings.

How will your hair look on the day that you beat depression? Are you going to treat yourself to all your favorite things like a massage, shopping spree, or manicure and pedicure? Keep this visualization close. Know that you are capable of using your breath to control your depression.

Breathe in deeply for a 5 count this time: 1, 2, 3, 4, 5. Breathe out and let your breath go out deeply: 1, 2, 3, 4, 5.

On the count of three, we will bring the meditation to a close. If you need to continue to meditate, feel free to do so. We are in no rush to get you to the next activity. Being mindful is all about taking your time to be present and aware of the moment on your own terms. You can go at your own pace. When you are ready, gently open your eyes. One. Two. Three.

Mindfulness Meditation for Insomnia

Before you begin, lie in a comfortable position on a soft surface like your bed, blanket, or couch. Play relaxing music in the background. Once you're comfortable and you're warm begin to concentrate on your breath.

From the deepest part of your stomach, breathe in. Then empty all the air out by opening your mouth and let all the air leave. You do not want a single ounce of air left in your body. Then you want to breathe in again. Repeat this step by slowly filling up your body with as much air as you can. Hold the breath for 3 seconds and then let it out for the count of three as well. Do this breath cycle 4 more times.

Breathe in. And breathe out. Feel like your limbs have just done a very intense workout and you are tired. Your legs and arms are tense and heavy. Your body aches from such an intense workout and you are tired. The only thing you want is to pile into your bed and go to sleep. You want to feel the rejuvenation of sleep to help your aching bones feel better.

Inhale and then exhale. Imagine that you have just had a full cup of warm feeling. Feel how warm your stomach is from the warm liquid as it sloshes in your belly, calming you and bringing you to sleep's shore. The warm, sweet milk makes you feel human and connects you to this month just like your breathing.

Breathe in deeply. Then breathe out just as deeply. Feel that you are in a long car ride taking a long windy road in the middle of nowhere. The road is long and windy, but the scenery is beautiful, and you are in the passenger seat enjoying how long the ride is. Your feet are handing in the dashboard and your window is slightly cracked. You feel the breeze going against your face and you are

Inhale from your diaphragm. Then exhale from just as deep in your diaphragm. Feel how your breath is causing your body to feel groggy and restless. Feel that your body is losing your alertness that you normally have through the day and feel the groggy calm that's overtaking your body.

If you think about any thoughts that interrupting your focus on breathing, gently move them out the way. Now we want to relax your body, so it feels nice and warm and activates your sleep trigger. Imagine you have just eaten a full meal and your stomach is full and plump. You are tired and groggy from a meal of eating all of your favorite foods.

As you breathe, try to feel any tension in your body so your breath can help you release the tension. To begin, we want to start at the head. Squint your eyes as close as possible and then open them until you feel relaxed.

Next, roll your neck from side to side. Put your chin down to your chest and then put your head on the floor. As you do this, feel the tension leave in your body, and in its place feel a nice comfortable, relaxed feeling. Move to your chest breathing as deeply as possible and breathe out. Then focus on your thighs and your legs keep going. You feel a nice warm feeling replacing it.

Next, we're going to feel like all of our anxiety has just disappeared. We're floating on clouds. The clouds wrap you like a blanket and a magic genie. Just keep flying and flowing into your going slowly into sleepland.

Next, we want to feel like we are at your favorite fishing spot or your favorite place in the mountains. The fish are biting at the surface of the lake and in the process making beautiful ripples that keep spreading wider and wider. As you are in the mountains, feel the heat of your body as you are snuggled deeply. You're your snowsuit. When you're in your place, you do not have to worry about going anywhere you are exactly where you need to be.

Breathe in and breathe out. Whatever your thoughts are, let them dissolve away and just focus on your breath. You do not have a set time that you have to be anywhere. There's no pressure to arrive.

Just feel safe and the warmth of being in the clouds. We do not have a care in the world. This is what it feels like. Feel that you are bouncing from cloud to cloud to cloud. You're just floating amongst the airy, pale blue skies. All of the tickles from the cloud are making your tired.

Do one more deep breath and then feel your entire body relax. Feel your arms and legs loosen. Feel your stomach and back gently move back and forth with every soft breath that you take. Feel each breath pushing you to a deep, peaceful sleep.

Keep your eyes closed and feel like a breath in the middle of hibernation. Nothing will be able to wake you up. You are going to rest deeply and peacefully. Just follow your breath until you go to sleep.

Then let the music guide you to the land of slumber.

Mindfulness Meditation for Grief and Loss

This mindfulness meditation is to help you cope with the pain and suffering from grief and loss. Be sure that you are in a comfortable place before we begin. That comfortable place could be sitting in a dignified position in a chair or lying down.

Have a pen and paper handy in case you need to write down anything later. Place your head in a comfortable position, and make sure your body is relaxed. Raise your shoulders up and hold them up before 5 seconds. Then let your shoulders release go and release all the tension out your body. You can also play soft, calming music in the background if you'd like. Take three deep breaths breathing from the very depths of your diaphragm and breathing out through your nose.

Breathe in. Breathe out. Still your thoughts. You are in a judgment-free zone.

Inhale for three counts: 1, 2, 3. And exhale for three counts: 1, 2, 3.

Inhale one more time. Exhale one more time.

Once you feel comfortable, if you feel the painful thoughts come back, that's okay. Do not try to fix the pain. Do not try to deal with the pain. Just feel it.

Breathe in deeply. If you want to cry, feel free to cry. If it feels like you will never ever get over this pain, breathe and brace that feeling filled up with all your pain. You will get over it.

Now take a breath and let the air fully out. Breathe in deeply again. Look at your thoughts neutrally. Now try to look at yourself like you're from the outside looking in. If you could describe yourself, what would it be? What's one good thing that you see about yourself? What's one area of opportunity? What can you learn from this situation?

Where do you feel the most pain? Is it in the middle of your chest or is it in the pit of your stomach? Wherever it is, zone in on your pain. Now that you've located that pain, take in a big breath and feel that the oxygen is healing the pain.

Next, imagine how your loved one will feel. Do you think they will want you to feel this way? If you can hear their voice one more time, what do you think they would say to you? Just listen to their voice and write it down for later. If you do not hear anything, except silence in your breath, that's okay as well.

As you inhale, take in the love that you know you have for the person and exhale then tension out. Feel grounded in this moment and know that things are going to be better. Grief does not last always. The more you breathe in, the more you grow. The more you breathe in, the less grief you have. Ride the wave of breath into calmness.

Know that your loved one is protecting you. Know that they're protecting you. Send love to them and know that the love is reciprocated. You are one in spirit and in mind. They are guiding you and sending rays of warmth, love and positive energy to you so that you know that you are not alone.

Feel the relaxation coming over you. Do not run away from the emotion. Now instead of feeling like the sadness, focus on the good times. The fun, the laughter, the realness. Take more deep breaths and bring energy into your body. Know that you're never alone. Replenish your broken heart with breaths and with positive affirmations.

Breathe in and then breathe out. Repeat after me, "I am loved." You are loved by yourself, and you are loved by your loved one. The pain you are feeling shows that someone loved you and you loved someone too.

Breathe in and then breathe out. Repeat after me. "I had precious valuable time with my loved one, and I know that I will get through this." The old cliché is true: 'Time heals all wounds.'

Breathe in and then breathe out. Repeat after me. "I know that grief and pain will not last forever." Just like anxiety, just like pain from hitting your big toe on the side of the bed, pain is temporary and one day you will not even feel the pain.

Breathe in and then breathe out. Repeat after me. "I know that the lessons and time I spend with the loved one will help me make it." Think about the words that you learned from your loved one. Let those words comfort you like your favorite blanket.

Breathe in and then breathe out. Repeat after me: "I am wiser, stronger, and I am ready for whatever lies ahead." You are strong, brave, kind and tough. You will get through this.

Breathe in and then breathe out. Hold the in-between space between your next breath. Now breathe in and breath out one more time.

On three, gently open your eyes and awaken. Keep the feelings of love, calmness, and feelings of happiness with you throughout the day.

In conclusion, this chapter continued to build on the previous chapter by giving you guided meditation scripts to use that target specific issues that you may be experiencing like stress, depression, grief, or insomnia. Each scripted meditation uses a combination of breathing, relaxation and visualization techniques to guide you through each session. Feel free to use them as is or modify each meditation as you see fit. You can use each one as a basis to build your own meditations as well. Remember, every time you meditate you improves, so please continue to practice.

Conclusion

"Be where you are, otherwise you will miss your life." – Buddha

Thank you for making it through to the end of Mindfulness Meditation: A Practical Guide for Beginners, let's hope it was informative and able to provide you with all of the tools you need to achieve your goals whatever they may be. If you can only take one thing away from this book, please take this, please know that mindfulness can transform your life. If can be the difference between a regular life or a life that's appreciated and full of gratitude. If you are on the track to being more mindful in your everyday life, know that you are on a journey that will unleash wonderful surprises in your life.

The next step is to find your special place so you can begin your mindful meditation practice. You can even go ahead and create your list of affirmations that you can use throughout your sessions. You can revisit any of your special phrases in the book that you marked to check out at any other time. Feel free to join any support group that can help answer any questions you may have along the way. There are great resources to check out online. You can also check out location meditation groups on Craigslist or find a Meetup site. Also, try to eat healthily and sleep well. The better you take care of your body, the better your meditation session will be. Overall health also helps you to be more mindful in your day-to-day life.

Remember, that you do not have to do everything right the right time when you meditate. As you progress in your practice, you will continue to improve. Embrace the journey. Lastly, do not stop learning. This book about: *Mindfulness and Meditation* is a great foundation to have, but continue to build on it. Continue to learn more about how the benefits of mindfulness meditation affect you. You can also continue to work on meditation by using guided meditations until you are at the point where you can do the meditations on your own without the help of guided meditations. This journey is to last a lifetime and the more prepared you are the more you will be prepared to sustain and improve your mindfulness meditation practice along the way.

Thank you.

www.ingramcontent.com/pod-product-compliance
Lightning Source LLC
Chambersburg PA
CBHW021130080526
44587CB00012B/1214